REGISTER OF TESTAMENTS

ABERDEEN

Three Parts in One

Part One: 1715-1734
Part Two: 1735-1759
Part Three: 1760-1800

Compiled by

Frances McDonnell

CLEARFIELD

Originally published by Frances McDonnell
St. Andrews, Scotland, 1997

Reprinted for Clearfield Company
Three Parts in One
by Genealogical Publishing Company
Baltimore, Maryland
2010

ISBN 978-0-8063-5453-8

Made in the United States of America

REGISTER OF TESTAMENTS

ABERDEEN

Part One: 1715-1734

INTRODUCTION

Some of the most important sources of information on our ancestors are to be found in the form of testaments. These documents can be expected to reveal the name and designation of the deceased, normally the date of death, the executor, an inventory of assets, liabilities, debtors and creditors, and usually a will. Registers of Testaments are generally available from the late 16th century to the early 19th century, and these contain significant material of relevance to the family historian. It should, however, be noted that not everyone left a will, and of those made, not all found their way into the books of the Commissary Court.

Until the 1820s, testaments in Scotland were "confirmed", by various Commissariot Courts throughout the land. These Courts were based roughly on pre-Reformation dioceses boundaries. The Commissariot Court of Edinburgh was often used by Scots residing overseas. After the 1820s, documents were usually, but not exclusively, lodged in the local Sheriff Court, with Edinburgh continuing to be used by those living abroad.

Fire destroyed the early records of the Commisariot of Aberdeen, including testaments, and the surviving records date only from 1715. This publication is in essence an alphabetical listing of the testaments confirmed by the Commissary Court of Aberdeen for the period 1715 to 1734.

The documents relating to those listed in this booklet can be viewed at the Scottish Record Office, Edinburgh.

St Andrews
1997

REGISTER OF TESTAMENTS
ABERDEEN
1715-1734

ABELL, ELSPET, in Tillybin, widow of **James Duncan**, sometime
  shoemaker in the Hardgate of Aberdeen, 15 Nov 1733.
ABELL, JOHN, sometime in Lachentille, thereafter in Findrassie, 19 Jun
  1729.
ABERCROMBIE, ALEXANDER, Capt, of Glassaugh, 22 Jan and 15 Apr
  1730.
ABERDEEN, GEORGE, Earl of, 28 Jan and 1 Nov 1722, 24 Feb 1730, 3
  Dec 1731. See also Lady **Margaret Gordon**.
ABERDEEN, GEORGE, merchant in Old Aberdeen, 19 Feb 1726.
ABERDEEN, JAMES, in Bailliestoun of Dyce, see **Agnes Taylor**.
ABERNETHY, JOHN, tenant in Auchipp, see **Robert Howie.**
ABOYNE, JOHN, Earl of, 13 Oct 1732.
ADAMSON, GEORGE, sometime in Tarwathie, 12 May 1727.
ADIE, JOHN, in Kirktoun of Cushny, sometime in Renniskillie, 29 May
  1722.
ADIE, JOHN, son to late **John A**, sometime in 29 Jun 1722.
ADIE, MARY, wife to **George Durrat**, merchant in Aberdeen, 14 Nov
  1724.
AIRTH, JOHN, sometime in Brousterbog, see **Elspet Nicoll.**
AITKINE, JOHN, in Broadtree of Concraig, 17 Jul 1734.
AITKINE, WILLIAM, salmon-fisher on Dee, 20 Sep 1722.
ALEXANDER, ALEXANDER, of Jackstoun, 11 Nov 1731.
ALEXANDER, BARBARA, only lawful daughter to the late **Patrick A**,
  merchant in Aberdeen, 1 Dec 1730.
ALEXANDER, PATRICK, see **Barbara Alexander**.
ALEXANDER, THOMAS, Mr, late minister at Logie Collstone, 16 Dec
  1731.
ALLAN, JAMES, merchant in Aberdeen, see **Janet Miller.**
ALLAN, JANET, in Poole-end, 20 Apr 1722.
ALLAN, JOHN, sometime in Blackblair, 29 Jan 1730.

1

ALLAN, WILLIAM, in Midtack of Rosehall, 7 Jan 1725.

ALLANACH, JEAN, widow of **Duncan Grierson**, sometime in Auchinskink, 31 Jan 1723.

ALLARDICE, HELEN, widow of **Alexander Cuming**, sometime of Culter, 2 Nov 1725.

ALLARDICE, JEAN, daughter of the late **John A**, late provost of Aberdeen, 3 Jun 1729.

ALLARDICE, JOHN, sometime provost of Aberdeen, 15 Jul 1722. See also **Jean Smart**.

ALLARDICE, MARGARET, widow of **John Logie**, merchant in Aberdeen, 2 Dec 1725.

ALLARDICE, THOMAS, son of the late **John A**, late provost of Aberdeen, 3 Jun 1729.

ANDERSON, ALEXANDER, in Knocksoul, 9 Nov 1721.

ANDERSON, ALEXANDER, in Arradoul, 15 Aug 1727.

ANDERSON, ALEXANDER, of Bourtie, 18 May 1728.

ANDERSON, ALEXANDER, in Logie Coldstone, 4 Feb 1732.

ANDERSON, CHRISTIAN and ISOBELL, daughters to late **James A**, wright, burgess of Aberdeen, 23 Jan 1728.

ANDERSON, ELIZABETH, widow of **John Mackie**, portioner in Inverury, 22 Sep 1724.

ANDERSON, JAMES, shoemaker in Old Aberdeen, 27 Jun 1724 and 23 Mar 1725.

ANDERSON, JAMES, wright, burgess of Aberdeen, 7 Dec 1725.

ANDERSON, JOHN, of Bourty, 6 Dec 1732.

ANDERSON, JOHN, at Mill of Barns, 11 Dec 1734.

ANDERSON, PETER, in Moss-side of Kingswells, 11 Feb 1729.

ANGUS, GEORGE, of Crofthead, 20 Oct 1733.

ANGUS, JOHN, Mr, minister at Kinnellar, 12 Mar (May) 1726.

ARBUTHNOT, NATHANIEL, in Rora, 26 Jun 1724.

ARCHIBALD, ALEXANDER, in Milltoun of Murtle, 15 Jul 1734.

BAIRD, JANET, Mrs, widow of **Alexander Paterson**, armourer, burgess of Aberdeen, 19 Mar 1723.

BAIRD, WILLIAM, of Achmeden, 1 Aug 1726 and 8 Jun 1730.

BAIRD, WILLIAM, late bailie of Cullen, see **Helen Ord**.

BANFF, GEORGE, Lord, 28 Jan 1723.

BANNERMAN, ALEXANDER, Sir, of Elsick, 5 Dec 1729.

BARBER, ALEXANDER, in Pitgair, 25 Mar 1726.

BARCLAY, HARRY, in Auchmull, 2 Jul 1733.

BARTLET, JAMES, merchant in Aberdeen, 12 Jun 1722.

BARTLET, JAMES, at Nether Mill of Auchmedden, 29 Jun 1732.

BAXTER, WILLIAM, late bailie in Old Aberdeen, 4 Oct 1725.

BETHE, JAMES, in Duniedeir, 13 Jan 1727.

BEVERLY, CHRISTIAN, wife of **John Boyes**, shipmaster in Aberdeen, 14 Sep 1727.

BIRNIE, ALEXANDER, merchant in Old Aberdeen, 22 Sep 1733.

BIRSS, JOHN, son of **Francis B**, sometime in Dykehead of Borrowstoun, 31 Dec 1723.

BISSET, ISABEL, widow of **John Drummond**, shipmaster in Fraserburgh, 1 Feb 1729 (1728).

BISSET, ISABELL, see **George Smith**.

BLACK, ALEXANDER, in Lochintilly, 22 Jul 1725.

BLACK, ALEXANDER, sub tenant in Mains of Cullin, 25 (May) Feb 1731.

BLACK, GILBERT, Mr, sometime of London, merchant, son of the late **Gilbert B**, bailie in Aberdeen, 26 Aug 1726 and 14 Jun 1728.

BLACK, ISOBELL, widow of **Robert Cuming**, merchant and late bailie of Aberdeen, 28 Jan 1730.

BLACK, JAMES, in Lachentilly, thereafter in Newtown of Skene, 24 Aug 1731.

BLACK, JOHN, miller at Upper Mill, 19 Jul 1723.

BLACK, MARGARET, in Old Aberdeen, 24 Jul 1725 (1724).

BLACKHALL, ANDREW, at Burn of Culter, 19 Sep 1729.

BLAYD, THOMAS, see **Marjorie Garrioch**.

BOOTH, JAMES, in Clintarty, and **Janet B**, his daughter, 5 Jul 1729.

BOOTH, JANET, see **James Booth**.

BOWER, WILLIAM, Mr, minister at Turriff, 1 Jul 1731.

BOWMAN, ALEXANDER, in Old Chaillach, 5 Aug and 15 Dec 1725.

BOYES, JOHN, shipmaster in Aberdeen, 25 Oct 1729. See **Christian Beverly**.

BRECK, ANDREW, sometime servant to John Leslie of Drumdollac, 1 Nov 1728. See **William Burnett**.

BROWN, ANDREW, sometime in Boghead, 23 Dec 1723.

BROWN, GEORGE, schoolmaster in Fordyce, 11 Oct 1732.

BROWN, GEORGE, shipmaster in Peterhead, 25 Feb 1734.

BROWN, GEORGE, merchant in Hattoun of Fintray, 18 Jan 1734.

BROWN, JOHN, of Neither Aslied, 21 Nov 1723.

BRUCE, GEORGE, armourer in Aberdeen, 6 Dec 1722.

BRUCE, JAMES, in Meikletoun of Slains, 6 Jun 1728.

BRUCE, WILLIAM, in Annachie, 16 Jan 1724.

BRUCE, WILLIAM, in Arbedie, 12 Jun 1730.

BRUCE, WILLIAM, sailor in Aberdeen, 27 Jul 1731.

BUCHAN, JAMES, Maj or Achmacoy, 13 Dec 1726.

BUCHAN, JOHN, Col, of Cairnbulg, 20 Jun 1728.

BURNET, ALEXANDER, in Upper Banchory, see **Janet Ridler**.

BURNET, ANDREW, of Elrick, 11 Jan 1722, see also Mrs **Marjory Johnston**.

BURNET, ANDREW, brother-german of Mr **Thomas B** of Kemnay, 8 Aug 1726 and 18 Jun 1730.

BURNET, BESSIE, widow of Mr **Alexander Ker**, sometime minister at Grange, 28 May 1728.

BURNET, JEAN, widow of Mr **Thomas Reid**, of Eslie, 30 Jul 1726.

BURNET, JOHN, Mr, minister of Monymusk, 3 Jun 1729.

BURNET, JOHN, junior, merchant in Aberdeen, 23 Nov 1731.

BURNET, ROBERT, senior, merchant in Aberdeen, 14 Mar 1727.

BURNET, THOMAS, dyer in Aberdeen, 14 Feb 1720.

BURNET, THOMAS, Mr, of Kemnay, 2 Jun 1730 and 8 Mar 1732.

BUTTER, MARGARET, widow of Mr **Walter Cochran** of Dumbreck, 24 Dec 1726.

BYRES, ROBERT, merchant in Dublin, see **Jean Sandilands**.

CAIRNY, JANET, in Meikle Findrassie, widow of **Gilbert Dun**, sometime in Nether Milnebuy of Skein, 12 Dec 1721 and 13 Jan 1726.

CAMPBELL, COLIN, Mr, minister of Aberdeen, 26 Sep 1728.

CAMPBELL, GEORGE, Mr, minister at Alva, Aug 1727.

CAMPBELL, MARGARET, widow of **Robert Grant** of Dunlugass, 13 Jul 1727.

CARNIE, JOHN, in Wester Millbuie, 21 Feb 1726.

CARNIE, WILLIAM, in Nether Afflock, 10 Mar 1726.

CATANACH, ARCHIBALD, sometime tenant in Newton of Balfad, 17 Nov 1730.

CATANACH, ELIZABETH, see **James Deuchar**, sometime in Bervie.

CATANACH, JAMES, sometime in Belnabodach, see **Marjory Ross**.

CATTO, ALEXANDER, in Craigietocher, 28 Feb 1724.

CHALMERS, JAMES, elder, in Drum of New Deer, 16 Jun 1725.

CHALMERS, PATRICK, sometime in Newseat, 17 Mar 1725.

CHALMERS, PATRICK, sometime merchant in Bridges, thereafter living in Balmad, 8 Nov 1726.

CHALMERS, PATRICK, Dr, physician in Aberdeen, 2 Dec 1727 and 23 Aug 1731, see also **Rachell Forbes**.

CHALMERS, WILLIAM, butcher in Seatoun, 27 Jun 1724.

CLARIHEW, ARTHUR, in Woodend, in Tillienetle, 29 Apr 1731.

CLARIHEW, WILLIAM, Mr, minister at Culsalmond, 15 Nov 1733.

CLARK, DONALD, in Kirktoun of Birss, 8 Aug 1723.

CLARK, HUGH, merchant in Bahiltock of Cabroch, 1 Oct 1724.

CLARK, JAMES, sometime at Little Milne of Esslemont, thereafter at Mill of Aden, 8 Jan 1722.

CLARK, JAMES, late bailie in Banff, 25 Jan 1728.

CLARK, ROBERT, merchant in Old Aberdeen, 5 Jul 1725.

CLYNE, JOHN, in Carnywhiny, see **Jeals Henderson.**

COCHRAN, JOHN, merchant in Aberdeen, 30 Sep 1723.

COCHRAN, WALTER, Mr, of Dumbreck, see **Margaret Butter.**

COCK, ISOBELL, widow of **William Strachan**, shoemaker in Banff, 18 Oct 1731.

COCK, PETER, shipmaster in Banff, 22 Feb 1728.

COLLIE, ALEXANDER, dyer in Cullen, 27 Sep 1723.

COLLIE, JOHN, of Belskevie, 2 Nov 1722.

COLLIE, WILLIAM, in Candeclirach, and **William C** his son, 20 Jan 1727.

COOK, PATRICK, Mr, minister, sometime residing at Auchiries, 30 Sep 1728.

COOK, THOMAS, in Kinclunie, 7 Sep 1721.

COOK, THOMAS, merchant in Banff, 11 Nov 1731.

COOK, WILLIAM, in Whitelay, 12 May 1731.

COOPER, ALEXANDER, master of the Music School of Aberdeen, 4 Oct 1722.

COOPER, ALEXANDER, in Knockespack, 27 Jun 1723.

COOPER, JAMES, smith in Banff, 14 Jun 1722.

COOPER, JAMES, merchant in Blacklaw of Tarves, 1 Apr 1731.

COOPER, WILLIAM, in Canahars, 28 Oct 1730.

COPLAND, WILLIAM, merchant in Mickendovie, 10 Apr 1730.

COUTS, ALEXANDER, in Ballachbuie, 5 Oct 1727.

COUTS, MARGARET, wife of **Thomas Steven**, in Easterbeltie, 24 Apr 1724.

COUTS, PETER, in Ballabeg, 12 Jan 1727.

CRAIG, JOHN, baker in Aberdeen, 20 Aug 1730.

CRAIK, JOHN, merchant in Fraserburgh, 25 Feb 1731.

CRUDEN, GEORGE, Mr, late Regent in the Marishall College of Aberdeen, 23 Mar 1724.

CRUDEN, WILLIAM, in Cairnhill, 8 Apr 1728.

CRUICKSHANK, ALEXANDER, sometime bailie in Peterhead, 20 Dec 1722.

CRUICKSHANK, GEORGE, late dean of guild of Aberdeen, 8 Apr 1724.

CRUICKSHANK, GEORGE, merchnt in Old Aberdeen, see **Barbara Finnie.**

CRUICKSHANK, WILLIAM, sometime in Logie Newtoun, 20 Feb 1729.

CUMING, ALEXANDER, in Hillock, 23 Feb 1722.

CUMING, ALEXANDER, of Blairinovinen (alias of Crimond), 30 Jul 1723 and 15 Feb (Jan) 1734.

CUMING, ALEXANDER, Sir, of Culter, 12 Apr and 5 May 1725 and 20 Jul 1726. See also **Helen Allardice.**

CUMING, CHARLES, second lawful son of **Gavin C** of Kinninmonth, 11 May 1728.

CUMING, DUNCAN, merchant in Aberdeen, 22 Dec 1725, see also **Jean Glass**.

CUMING, ELIZABETH, Dame, widow of Sir **Alexander C** of Culter, 16 Jan 1730.

CUMING, GAVIN, of Kinninmonth, 11 May 1728, see **Charles Cuming**.

CUMING, ROBERT, merchant in Aberdeen, 24 Feb 1727.

CUMING, ROBERT, merchant, and late bailie of Aberdeen, see **Isobell Black**.

CUMING, WILLIAM, see **William Moir**.

CUSHNIE, ALEXANDER, in Quhobs, 19 Dec 1733.

CUTHBERT, DONALD, late servant to Sir Alexander Burnet of Leyes, 20 Jul 1724.

DARG, ALEXANDER, Mr, in Gavill, 20 Feb 1729.

DARLING, PETER, Mr, late minister at Boyndie, 27 Jan 1731 and 11 Jun 1734.

DAVIDSON, ALEXANDER, Mr, of Newtown, 8 Dec 1732, see **Elspet D**.

DAVIDSON, ELSPET, daughter of Mr **Alexander D** of Newtoun, 24 Aug 1724.

DAVIDSON, GEORGE, of Cairnbrogie, 28 Apr 1726, 19 Jul 1734 and 28 Aug 1734.

DAVIDSON, GILBERT, farmer in Torrieburn, and **Christian Thomson**, his spouse, 23 Feb 1727.

DAVIDSON, JAMES, merchant in Aberdeen, 12 Feb 1734.

DAVIDSON, ROBERT, cooper, burgess of Aberdeen, 10 Dec 1723.

DEANS, ALEXANDER, Mr, minister at Birss, 8 Nov 1726.

DEANS, JOHN, merchant in Aberdeen, 25 Oct 1729.

DEUCHAR, JOHN, sometime in Bervie, and **Elizabeth Catanach**, his wife, 8 Feb 1724.

DEUCHAR, JOHN, at Mill of Garlogie, see **Barbara Walker**.

DEUCHAR, ROBERT, blacksmith in Cowhill, 15 Jun 1728.

DINGWALL, ARTHUR, of Brownhill, 18 Dec 1729, see also **Jean Chalmers**.

DINGWALL, WILLIAM, Mr, of Brucklaw, 28 Dec 1733.

DONALD, ROBERT, in Kirktoun of Banchory, 12 Feb 1726.

DONALDSON, JAMES, servant to Thomas Forbes, younger, of Echt, 18 Jan 1722.

DOUGLAS, ALEXANDER, merchant in Aberdeen, 7 Mar 1733.

DOUGLAS, JOHN, merchant in Aberdeen, 5 Jan 1723, 12 Oct 1725 and 29 Jan 1726.

DOUGLAS, ROBERT, Mr, of Blackmill, 15 Mar 1725.

DOWNIE, FRANCIS, Mr, tenant in Mains of Kemnay, see **Jean Orem**.

DOWNIE, MARGARET, wife of **John Forsyth**, in Cottoun of Pittodrie, 13 Jan 1724.

DOWNIE, ROBERT, in Glencoury, in Strathdone, 15 Feb 1722.

DRUMMOND, JOHN, shipmaster in Fraserburgh, see **Isobell Bisset**.

DRUMMOND, WILLIAM, late shipmaster in Fraserburgh, 16 Nov 1727.

DUFF, ALEXANDER, gardener in Kildrummie, 15 Oct 1723.

DUFF, ALEXANDER, baker in Aberdeen, 6 Feb 1728.

DUFF, GEORGE, of Stockbrigg, see **Catherine Williamson**.

DUFF, JOHN, messenger in Aberdeen, 30 Jul 1724 and 22 Jun 1731.

DUGUID, CHARLES, in Kirktoun of Strathdon, 5 Feb 1730.

DUGUID, FRANCIS, of Auchinhove, 18 Jan 1721.

DUN, ELIZABETH, widow of Mr **Adam Sutherland**, late parson of Duffus, 9 Jul 1724.

DUN, GILBERT, sometime in Nether Millbuy of Skein, see **Janet Cairny**.

DUN, ISOBELL, in Craigievar, 3 May 1732.

DUNBAR, ALEXANDER, Mr, of Munkshill, late tenant at the Miln of Tiftie, 3 Mar 1724.

DUNBAR, JAMES, at Miln of Rethen, 1 Mar 1728.

DUNCAN, ALEXANDER, shipmaster in Banff, 2 Mar 1731.

DUNCAN, JAMES, in Quartans, 10 Aug 1731.

DUNCAN, JAMES, sometime shoemaker in Hardgate of Aberdeen, see **Elspet Abell**.

DUNCAN, JOHN, in Peterhead, 7 Nov 1727.

DUNCAN, JOHN, in Kincardine O'Neill, 20 Jun 1734.

DUNCAN, WILLIAM, in Drumfork, 19 Jun 1733.

DURRAT (DURWARD), GEORGE, merchant in Aberdeen, see **Mary Adie.**

DURWARD, NORMAN, merchant in Aberdeen, see **Marjory Gibb**.

DYCE, WILLIAM, Mr, minister at Belhelvie, 2 Jun 1727.

EDWARD, ALEXANDER, in Dyckeside, 9 Oct 1724.

EDWARD, JAMES, in Letter of Skene, see **Margaret Smith**.

EGO, THOMAS, sometime in Haughhead, see **Margaret Fiddes**.

ELLIS, JAMES, merchant in Banff, 24 May 1733.

ELLIS, WILLIAM, in Sheills, parish of Belhelvie, 15 Feb 1733.

ELMSLIE, CHRISTIAN, see **James Wilson**.

ELMSLIE, WILLIAM, in New Groddy, 8 Jun 1733.

ERSKINE, WILLIAM, of Pittodrie, 28 Feb 1724.

FARQUHAR, JAMES, Mr, minister at Coull, 18 Apr 1734.

FARQUHAR, ROBERT, Mr, schoolmaster at Banchory-Ternan, 4 Nov 1731.

FARQUHAR, WILLIAM, in Banchory-Ternan, 14 May 1731.

FARQUHARSON, ALEXANDER, surgeon, brother to **Robert F** of Finzean, 10 Feb 1725.

FARQUHARSON, ALEXANDER, younger of Achindrine, eldest son of **Lewis F**, of A, 17 Nov 1727.

FARQUHARSON, ALEXANDER, in Corse, 30 Nov 1731.

FARQUHARSON, ARTHUR, Mr, of Cults, 9 Dec 1725.

FARQUHARSON, CHARLES, see **Elizabeth Farquharson**.

FARQUHARSON, ELIZABETH, widow of **Charles F**, late of Monaltry, 25 Jul 1723.

FARQUHARSON, FINDLAY, of Cults, see **Anne Leith**.

FARQUHARSON, HARRY, of Whytehouse, 15 May 1724.

FARQUHARSON, ROBERT, see **Alexander Farquharson**.

FAUS, JOHN, at Bridge of Gairden, 16 Jul 1730.

FERGUSON, ALEXANDER, of Tombelly, see **Eupham McHardie**.

FERGUSON, ALEXANDER, farmer in Old Aberdeen, see **Isobell Stephen**.

FERGUSON, JANET, sometime in Inverurie, widow of **John Wishart**, sometime in Old Meldrum, 25 Jul 1734.

FERGUSON, JOHN, see **Janet Smith**.

FERGUSON, WALTER, sometime bailie in Inverurie, 21 Jan 1729.

FIDDES, MARGARET, in Haughhead, widow of **Thomas Ego**, sometime in Haughhead, 26 Feb 1734.

FINDLATER, JOHN, see **Margaret Findlater**.

FINDLATER, MARGARET, lawful daughter of the late Mr **John F**, sometime master of the Grammar School of Aberdeen, 18 Dec 1730.

FINNIE, BARBARA, widow of **George Cruickshank**, merchant in Old Aberdeen, 25 Jun 1726.

FORBES, ALEXANDER, of Ballogie, 23 Dec 1721, see **Jean Forbes** and **Elizabeth Forbes**.

FORBES, ALEXANDER, and ELIZABETH, children to **John F**, merchant in Aberdeen, 26 Jun 1722.

FORBES, ALEXANDER, of Invernochtie, 12 Nov 1725.

FORBES, ALEXANDER, sometime tidesman in Aberdeen, see **Elizabeth Geddes**.

FORBES, ALEXANDER, of Barn, late tidewaiter at Inverness, 24 Nov 1730.

FORBES, ALEXANDER, see **Arthur Forbes**.

FORBES, ARCHIBALD, Mr, of Putachie, 18 Feb 1727.

FORBES, ARTHUR, in Tolmads, son of the late **Alexander F**, of Invernochty, 20 Jan 1726.

FORBES, ARTHUR, in Tillieriach, 8 Dec 1726.

FORBES, ARTHUR, of Echt, 1 Nov 1728.

FORBES, CHARLES, of Camfield, 25 Jul 1728.

FORBES, DAVID, of Leslie, 15 Jun 1727.

FORBES, ELIZABETH, daughter of the late **Alexander Forbes** of Ballogie, 23 Dec 1729.

FORBES, ELIZABETH, see **Alexander Forbes**.

FORBES, FRANCIS, Capt, Sheriff-Substitute of Aberdeen, 4 Feb and 21 Mar 1724 and 14 Feb 1728.

FORBES, GEORGE, of Midmiln of Cruden, 5 Jun 1728.

FORBES, GEORGE, senior, merchant in Aberdeen, 28 Apr 1730.

FORBES, GEORGE, of Skellater, 12 May 1731.

FORBES, GEORGE, of Sheills, 28 Jan 1731.

FORBES, GEORGE, in Bomakessie, 15 Feb 1733.

FORBES, ISOBELL, lawful daughter to late **William F** of Invernochtie, younger, 8 Dec 1726.

FORBES, JAMES, merchant in Turriff, 31 Mar 1733.

FORBES, JEAN, wife of **John Wemyss**, in Aberdour, 13 Jan 1722.

FORBES, JEAN, widow of **Alexander F**, of Ballogie, 11 Jun 1724.

FORBES, JOHN, of Inverernan, 31 Jul 1722.

FORBES, JOHN, in Keithback, 21 Jul 1727.

FORBES, JOHN, sometime collector of the cess of Aberdeenshire, 1 Nov 1733.

FORBES, JOHN, Mr, minister at Slains, 13 Dec 1733.

FORBES, JOHN, see **Alexander Forbes**.

FORBES, NATHANIEL, of Ledmacay, 15 Jul 1728.

FORBES, PATRICK, shipmaster in Aberdeen, see **Christian Smith**.

FORBES, PATRICK, of Killermont, 31 Aug 1732.

FORBES, PETER, in uniedeer, see **Elspet Reid**.

FORBES, RACHELL, widow of Dr **Patrick Chalmers**, MD, in Aberdeen, 2 Sep 1731.

FORBES, WILLIAM, Lord, and Lady **Anne F**, 7 May 1723.

FORBES, WILLIAM, Sir, of Craigivar, 24 Dec 1723 and 3 Nov 1727. See also Dame **Margaret Rose**.

FORDYCE, BARBARA, widow of **George French**, dyer in Aberdeen, 9 May 1728.

FORDYCE, GEORGE, merchant and late Provost of Aberdeen, 5 Jun 1733.

FORSYTH, JOHN, in Cottoun of Pittodry, see **Margaret Downie.**

FOWLER (FOULLAR), JANET, in Endovie, 17 May 1728.

FRASER, ALEXANDER, glover, burgess in Aberdeen, 6 Sep 1728.

FRASER, ANNE, widow of **Robert Lyon**, sometime in Damehill, thereafter in Midlemure of Belhelvie, 3 Feb 1730.

FRASER, CHARLES, Lord, 25 Mar 1730.

FRASER, FRANCIS, in Burnside of Lumphanan, 9 Feb 1727.

FRASER, GEORGE, Mr, sub-principal of the King's College of Aberdeen, 2 Sep 1727.

FRASER, JAMES, of Streichen, 4 Jan 1726.

FRASER, JAMES, Mr, of Lonmay, 22 Jul 1730.

FRASER, JAMES, in Tillieve, 11 Jun 1731.

FRASER, JEAN, widow of late **Robert Irvine**, of Fedderet, 15 Jul 1728.

FRASER, JEAN, widow of **Robert Smith**, merchant in Peterhead, 9 Nov 1732.

FRASER JOHN, senior, merchant in Aberdeen, 12 Apr 1727.

FRASER, JOHN, in Mains of Cairnbulg, 30 Mar 1733.

FRASER, KATHARINE ANNE, Lady, widow of Mr **William F** of Fraserfield, advocate, 19 Apr 1734.

FRASER, WILLIAM, Mr, of Fraserfield, 24 Feb 1729 and 19 Jun 1734, see Lady **Katharine Anne Fraser**.

FRASER, WILLIAM, merchant in Aberdeen, see **Margaret Jaffray**.

FRASER, WILLIAM, of Inverallachie, 4 May 1733.

FRENCH, GEORGE, dyer in Aberdeen, see **Barbara Fordyce**. See also **Isabell** and **James F**.

FRENCH, ISABELL, lawful daughter of **George F**, sometime dyer in Aberdeen, 24 Dec 1734.

FRENCH, JAMES, second son of **George F**, dyer, burgess of Aberdeen, 3 Feb 1732.

FYFE (FIFE), ALEXANDER, in Grodie, and **Agnes Nicol**, his wife, 22 (Jun) Jan 1727.

GALLOWAY, ALEXANDER, in Caden, 22 Dec 1733.

GARDEN, ALEXANDER, of Troup, 19 Nov 1731.

GARDEN, GEORGE, Dr, minister in Aberdeen, 16 Feb 1733.

GARDEN, POOR JAMES, in Toux, 2 Jun 1724.

GARRIOCH, MARJORIE, in Bythnie, widow of **Thomas Blayd**, maltman in Perth, 20 Feb 1729.

GATHERER, JAMES, Mr, minister in Old Aberdeen, 31 Jul 1733.

GEDDES, ELIZABETH, widow of **Alexander Forbes**, sometime tidesman in Aberdeen, 13 Mar 1728.

GEDDES, JOHN, merchant in Banff, 20 Nov 1721.

GELLAN, MARY, servant to Mr Martine Shank, minister at Banchory-Ternan, 6 Jun 1728.

GELLAN, ROBERT, late butcher, burgess of Aberdeen, see **Margaret Ross**.

GELLIE, ALEXANDER, Mr, late parson of Fordyce, 5 Dec 1722.

GELLIE, ELIZABETH, widow of **John Hall**, merchant in Aberdeen, 28 May and 14 Jun 1723.

GELLIE, HELEN, widow of **Alexander Forbes**, of Blackford, 18 Jan 1732.

GELLIE, MARGARET, widow of **Andrew Ross**, of Balblair, 30 Oct 1730.

GELLIE, WILLIAM, late Dean of Guild of Aberdeen, 18 Jun 1724 and 3 Aug 1727.

GERARD, WILLIAM, in Culbyth, 30 Jul 1734.

GIBB, MARJORY, widow of **Norman Durward**, merchant in Aberdeen, 6 Jun 1734.

GIBBON, WILLIAM, sometime in Knowhead, and **Helen Stewart**, his wife, 27 Jan 1726.

GLASS, JEAN, widow of **Duncan Cuming**, merchant in Aberdeen, 5 Feb 1729.

GLENNY, JAMES, in Mains of Echt, 18 May 1727.

GORDON, ADAM, in Newtoun of Corynassie, 31 Dec (1720) 1724.

GORDON, ADAM, of Inverebrie, 13 Aug 1726 (1725).

GORDON, ALEXANDER CLUNY, merchant in Aberdeen, 9 Aug 1722.

GORDON, ARCHIBALD, merchant at Portsoy, himself, and **William G**, of Tarskine, in trust, 10 Jul 1729.

GORDON, ARTHUR, Mr, see **Robert Gordon**.

GORDON, CHRISTIAN, resident in Old Meldrum, 15 Nov 1731.

GORDON, DUNCAN, merchant in Aberdeen, 9 Nov 1721.

GORDON, FRANCIS, of Craig, 14 May 1728 and 11 Apr 1729.

GORDON, FRANCIS, mason in Lumphannan, 6 Oct 1732.

GORDON, GEORGE, of Clastyrum, 21 Nov 1721.

GORDON, GEORGE, of Mill of Kincardine, 5 Jul 1722.

GORDON, GEORGE, merchant in Aberdeen, see **Christian Skene**.

GORDON, GEORGE, Mr, of Rainieshill, 27 Aug and 11 Oct 1731.

GORDON, GEORGE, at Bridgend of Deer, 6 Sep 1733.

GORDON, GEORGE, Dr, physician in Banff, 20 Sep 1733.

GORDON, GEORGE, merchant in Old Aberdeen, 12 Dec 1734.

GORDON, ISABELL, widow of **George Shepherd**, tailor, burgess of Aberdeen, 10 Aug 1728.

GORDON, JAMES, Dr, younger of Fechill, 6 Jan 1724 and 15 Sep 1730, see also **Margaret Baird**.

GORDON, JAMES, at Miln of Achindore, and **Margaret Strachan**, his wife, 28 Apr 1726.

GORDON, JAMES, of Auchlyne, 3 Feb 1730.

GORDON, JAMES, chapman of Fyvie, 19 Aug 1730.

GORDON, JAMES, shipmaster in Fraserburgh, 27 Dec 1732.

GORDON, JEAN, widow of **George Lumsden**, sometime in Mill of Waterfoull, thereafter wife to ...... Hay, of Rainestoun, 12 Mar 1724.

GORDON, JOHN, of Tilliechoydie, 8 Jan 1722.
GORDON, JOHN, Mr, minister of Old Deer, 26 Jan 1722.
GORDON, JOHN, of Nethermuir, 15 May 1725 and 18 Apr 1733.
GORDON, JOHN, of Acluchries, see **Elizabeth Grant**.
GORDON, JOHN, of Fechell, 22 Sep 1730 and 12 Aug 1731.
GORDON, JOHN, late baillie of Aberdeen, 5 Dec 1732.
GORDON, JOHN, son of **John G**, late baillie of Aberdeen, 5 Dec 1732.
GORDON, MARGARET, widow of **James Keith** of Crichie, 5 Dec 1728
    and 20 Sep 1733.
GORDON, NATHANIEL, of Noth, 16 Aug 1722 and 11 Feb 1724.
GORDON, ROBERT, Mr, minister at Rathven, 8 Aug 1724.
GORDON, ROBERT, Mr, of Cluny, advocate, 1 Nov 1729, 11 and 13 Dec
    1732.
GORDON, ROBERT, only lawful son of the late Mr **Arthur G**, advocate,
    12 Jun 1731.
GORDON, THOMAS, in Strathhead, 9 Dec 1729.
GORDON, WALTER, tidesman at Banff, 10 Mar 1725.
GORDON, WILLIAM, in Buthlaw, 8 Feb 1722.
GORDON, WILLIAM, see **Archibald Gordon**.
GOW, JEAN, wife of late **James Seton**, sometime at Mill of Gilkomstone,
    thereafter at Oldrain, 22 Oct 1734.
GRANT, ALLAN, in Ardowny, 5 Jun 1732.
GRANT, ELIZABETH, widow of **John Gordon** of Acluchries, 15 Mar
    1728.
GRANT, MARGARET, widow of **Alexander Reid**, tailor, burgess of
    Aberdeen, 6 Feb 1722.
GRANT, ROBERT, of Dunlugass, see **Margaret Campbell**.
GRANT, WILLIAM, in Ardfork, 10 Mar 1732.
GRAY, AGNES, see Capt **John Stewart**.
GRAY, ALEXANDER, at Lightwood, 11 Apr 1729.
GRAY, CHRISTIAN, in Dykeside, 16 Mar 1732.
GRAY, JAMES, in Longley, 15 Oct 1723.
GRAY, JOHN, armourer in Aberdeen, 2 Jun 1724.
GRAY, JOHN, merchant in Aberdeen, see **Katharine Irvine**.
GRAY, MARGARET, widow of **William Taylor**, merchant in Aberdeen, 24
    Feb 1733.
GRAY, ROBERT, Mr, minister of the Gospel, 26 Nov 1730.
GREGORY, GREGOR, merchant in Aberdeen, 16 Mar 1723.
GREIG, JOHN, merchant in Old Aberdeen, 23 Sep 1724.
GRIERSON, DUNCAN, sometime in Auchinskink, see **Jean Allanach**.
GUTHRIE, ANDREW, Mr, minister at Peterhead, 12 Dec 1723 and 26
    Jun 1729.

HALKET, JOHN, in Mains of Gight, 23 Apr 1734.
HALKET, WALTER, in Templand, 13 Nov 1733.
HALL, ANDREW, butcher in Forresterhall, 17 Jun 1724.
HALL, JOHN, merchant in Aberdeen, see **Elizabeth Gellie**.
HAMILTON, JAMES, of Cowbardie, 19 Feb 1728,
HARDIE, THOMAS, in Stonybank, 6 Aug 1728.
HARVIE, ALEXANDER, in Patiesmill, parish of Keithhall, 5 Nov 1730.
HARVIE, GILBERT, merchant in Aberdeen, 3 Jan 1734.
HARVIE, PATRICK, Mr, of Mamevlaw, late minister at Forgue, see **Margaret Scougall**.
HARVIE, ROBERT, Mr, of Mameulay, see **Janet Seton**.
HAY, ..., see **Jean Gordon**.
HAY, ADAM, Mr, minister at Montquhiter, 14 Aug 1729.
HAY, ALEXANDER, of Rannistoun, 16 Nov 1721.
HAY, ALEXANDER, tenant in Lumphard, 30 Jun 1730.
HAY, ALEXANDER, late burgess of Cullen, see **Anna Ogilvie**.
HAY, ANDREW, of Asleid, 6 Nov 1723.
HAY, JOHN, see **William Hay**.
HAY, WALTER, of Licklyhead, 10 Dec 1725.
HAY, WILLIAM, sometime in Muldavid, and **John H**, thereafter his eldest son, 12 Nov 1724.
HECTOR, JAMES, in Burnhead of Birss, 5 Nov 1730.
HENDERSON, ANDREW, in Oldtown of Inveray, 16 Apr 1731.
HENDERSON, JEALS, wife to **John Clyne**, in Carnywhiny, 13 Sep 1723.
HENDRY, JOHN, at Walkmiln of Clunie, 4 Feb 1731.
HEPBURN, ALEXANDER, merchant in Aberdeen, ... 1724.
HOG, JAMES, merchant in Aberdeen, second son of the late **James H** of Ramoir, 6 Aug 1725.
HOG, WILLIAM, Mr, son of the late **James H** of Ramoir, 19 Feb 1730.
HOWIE, ROBERT, and **John Abernethy**, tenants in Auchipp, belonging to James, Lord Deskford, 3 Sep 1724.
HUNTER, ALEXANDER, sometime in Tillinturk, thereafter in Leyhead of Lumwhanan, 20 Aug 1722.
HUNTER, ALEXANDER, merchant in Aberdeen, 16 May 1733.
HUNTER, JAMES, Mr, chamberlane to the Earl of Aberdeen, 2 Jul 1723.
HUNTER, WILLIAM, Mr, minister in Banff, 13 Nov 1730.
HUTCHEON, ALEXANDER, in Hesselhead, 8 Nov 1733.
HUTCHEON, ANDREW, tailor in Aberdeen, 30 Dec 1726.
HUTCHEON, JOHN, cowfeeder in Aberdeen, 14 Mar 1732.
IMRIE, ELSPET, in Dockenwall, 9 Jun 1726.
INGRAM, ALEXANDER, in Blackhillock, 31 Dec 1728.
INNES, GEORGE, Sir, of Coxtoun, 3 Sep 1723.

INNES, JAMES, of Lichnet, 19 Jun 1728.

INNES, JOHN, of Sinnahard, 15 Dec 1718 (1729) and 5 Dec 1728.

INNES, JOHN, of Culquoch, 15 Dec 1725.

INNES, JOHN, in Mains of Elrick, 7 Feb 1734.

INNES, MARY, widow of **Thomas Scott**, barber, burgess of Aberdeen, 7 Jul 1732.

INNES, PATRICK, of Socoth, 16 Dec 1725.

INNES, PATRICK, in Newburgh, 6 Nov 1734.

IRVINE, ALEXANDER, janitor in the King's College of Aberdeen, 23 Apr 1724.

IRVINE, ALEXANDER, see **Anne Irvine**.

IRVINE, ANNE, lawful daughter of the late **Alexander I** of Lenturk, 22 Jan 1730.

IRVINE, ARTHUR, sometime in Milntoun of Drum, 30 Sep 1728.

IRVINE, HELEN, daughter to late Mr **John I** of Saphock, 5 Apr 1727.

IRVINE, JEAN, Lady Drum, 9 Aug 1725.

IRVINE, JOHN, see **Helen Irvine**.

IRVINE, KATHARINE, widow of **John Gray**, merchant in Aberdeen, 9 Mar 1728.

IRVINE, ROBERT, of Fedderet, see **Jean Fraser**.

JACK, ROBERT, in Fintray, 14 Jun 1733.

JAFFRAY, MARGARET, widow of **William Fraser**, merchant in Aberdeen, 1 Dec 1730.

JAFFRAY, MARY, widow of **Gilbert Noble**, tydewaiter in Aberdeen, 16 Jun 1724.

JAMIESON, ARCHIE, see **John Jamieson**.

JAMIESON, JOHN, alias ARCHIE, in Birkhall, 10 Feb 1732.

JAMIESON, JOHN, in Nether Ord, 5 Feb 1729.

JOHNSTON, ALEXANDER, at Overmill of Cruden, 30 May 1723.

JOHNSTON, ALEXANDER, shipmaster in Aberdeen, 16 May 1724.

JOHNSTON, GEORGE, Mr, minister of Kingedward, 21 Sep 1733.

JOHNSTON, JEAN, widow of **James Smith**, gunsmith in Aberdeen, 31 Aug 1731.

JOHNSTON, JOHN, of Bishopstoun, 27 Dec 1728.

JOHNSTON, MARJORY, Mrs, widow of **Andrew Burnet** of Elrick, 2 Feb and 15 Nov 1726 and 18 Jan 1727.

JOHNSTON, ROBERT, resident in Aberdeen, 27 Apr 1725.

JOHNSTON, WILLIAM, Mr, minister at Premnay, 12 Dec 1732.

KEIR, WILLIAM, of Strathnethin, and **Beatrix McGregor**, his wife, 15 Oct 1723.

KEITH, ELIZABETH, see **Margaret Keith**.

KEITH, GEORGE, merchant in Fraserburgh, 10 Mar 1727.

KEITH, JANET, daughter of Mr **William K**, minister at Keithhall, 19 Dec 1723.

KEITH, JAMES, see **Margaret Gordon**.

KEITH, JAMES, see **Jean** and **Margaret Keith**.

KEITH, JEAN, daughter of late **James K**, of Keithfield, 8 Apr 1725.

KEITH, JOHN, see **Margaret Keith**.

KEITH, MARGARET, daughter of **James K** of Keithfield, 8 Apr 1725.

KEITH, MARGARET, JOHN and ELIZABETH, children of the late Mr **William K**, late minister at Keithhall, 20 Mar 1729.

KEITH, WILLIAM, see **Janet Keith**, also **Margaret, John** and **Elizabeth Keith**.

KEITH, WILLIAM, in Truffhill, 8 Jun 1725.

KELLIE, ALEXANDER, merchant in Aberdeen, 29 Mar 1734.

KEMP, JANET, in Fornet, 27 Nov 1725.

KEMP, JOHN, sometime in Brae of Balogie, see **Agnes Philp**.

KEMP, MARGARET, see **Patrick Kemp**.

KEMP, PATRICK and MARGARET, children of the late **John K**, in Braes of Balogie, 25 May 1732.

KENNEDY, JAMES, in Miltoun of Fyvie, 26 Nov 1734.

KENNEDY, JOHN, Mr, sometime minister at Peterculter, 9 Jan 1724, see also **Jean Irvine**.

KER, ALEXANDER, Mr, sometime minister at Grange, see **Bessie Burnet**.

KER, ANNE, daughter of **James K**, sometime in Mains of Killdrummy, 4 Jun 1724.

KER, ARTHUR, in Wester Clova, 12 Feb 1734.

KER, GEORGE, Mr, in Drumnahyde, 7 Jan 1725.

KER, JAMES, in Mains of Kildrummy, 4 Feb 1725.

KIDD, GEORGE, late tenant and possessor of the Walkmiln of Pladie, 24 Jan 1728.

KINNOUL, GEORGE, Earl of, see Lady **Jean Hay**.

LAMOND, DONALD, in Auchichiness, 25 Jul 1726.

LARGOE, JOSUA, dancing-master in Aberdeen, 18 Mar 1730.

LAUDER, ROBERT, of Rosecraig, 11 Mar 1723.

LAURIE, CHARLES, late treasurer of Aberdeen, 15 Dec 1727.

LEASK, ALEXANDER, Mr, minister within the presbytery of Turriff, 18 Jul 1730.

LEGERTWOOD, ISOBELL, widow of **Patrick Shand**, merchant in Aberdeen, 30 May and 2 Nov 1728.

LEGERTWOOD, JOHN, in Orchardtoun, 12 Jun 1722.

LEITH, ANN, widow of **Finlay Farquharson** of Cults, 12 Aug 1729.

LEITH, ELIZABETH, widow of **Alexander Lumsden** of Cushny, 17 Jun (1729) 1730.

LEITH, WILLIAM, of Oldwhat, 21 Dec 1731.

LEONARD, JAMES, weaver, burgess of Aberdeen, 7 Dec 1725.

LESLIE, CHARLES, in Walkerhill, 1 Feb 1729.

LESLIE, GEORGE, of Burdsbank, 1 Jun 1724.

LESLIE, GEORGE, of Balquhine, 18 Jan 1732 and 22 Dec 1733.

LESLIE, GILBERT, Mr, merchant in Aberdeen, 17 Mar 1725.

LESLIE, JOHN, late bailie of Aberdeen, 18 Sep 1730.

LESLIE, PATRICK, in Tocher, 11 Aug 1722.

LESLIE, PATRICK, hatmaker in Aberdeen, 29 Nov 1726.

LESLIE, PATRICK, Count of Balquhain, 24 Aug 1730 and 22 Dec 1733.

LESLIE, WILLIAM, Mr, minister at St Fergus, 8 Jul 1729.

LESSELL, ROBERT, in Lavlodge, 25 Jul 1728.

LEYS, WILLIAM, in Dawan, 25 Feb 1725.

LINDSAY, DAVID, Mr, late minister at Drumoak, 27 May 1724 and 4 Oct 1733.

LINDSAY, WILLIAM, of Culsh, 6 Jul 1722.

LITTLEJOHN, ALEXANDER, sometime in Rothie, 10 Jul 1724.

LITTLEJOHN, ANDREW, in Midletoun of Blackfoord, see **Isobell Paul**.

LITTLEJOHN, PATRICK, feuar in Old Meldrum, 21 Jul 1726.

LOGIE, JOHN, merchant in Aberdeen, see **Margaret Allardyce**.

LOWSON, HARRY, gardener in Banff, and **James** and **Patrick L**, his sons, 3 Sep 1729.

LOWSON, JAMES, see **Harry Lowson**.

LOWSON, PATRICK, see **Harry Lowson**.

LOWSON, PATRICK, merchant in Banff, 18 Oct 1722.

LUCKIE, JOHN, shoemaker in Spittell, 28 Feb 1724.

LUMSDEN, ALEXANDER, of Cushny, see **Elizabeth Leith**.

LUMSDEN, DAVID, of Cushny, 16 Apr 1730.

LUMSDEN, GEORGE, in Milne of Westercoul, 11 Jan 1722.

LUMSDEN, GEORGE, sometime in Mill of Waterfoull, see **Jean Gordon**.

LUMSDEN, JAMES, lawful son to **William L**, sometime in Titabouty, 7 May 1730.

LUMSDEN, JOHN, Mr, minister at Longside, 6 Apr 1731 (1732).

LUMSDEN, WILLIAM, in Titabutie, 28 Feb 1723.

LUMSDEN, WILLIAM, maltman, burgess of Aberdeen, 17 Mar 1725.

LUMSDEN, WILLIAM, see **James Lumsden**.

LYAL, JOHN, maltster in Aberdeen, 6 Dec 1733.

LYON, ROBERT, sometime in Damehill, thereafter in Midlemure of Belhelvie, see **Anne Fraser**.

McDUELL, THOMAS, late officer of Excise in Banff, 20 Jun 1729.

McGREGOR, BEATRIX, see **William Keir.**
McHARDIE, EDWARD, in Corriehoull, 18 Jun 1730.
McHARDIE, EUPHIAN, wife to **Alexander Ferguson**, of Tombelly, 2 Jul 1724.
MacHATTIE, JOHN, in Farnachlie, 5 Mar 1730.
McKADIE, ROBERT, sometime in Toldaquhili, 23 Jun 1730.
McKAILL, MATTHEW, Dr, physician in Aberdeen, 19 Mar 1734.
McSWEEN, DONALD, Mr, minister at Strathdon, 10 Feb 1732.
MACKIE, GEORGE, fuller at Monymusk, 3 Apr 1722.
MACKIE, ISOBELL, see **James Mackie.**
MACKIE, JAMES and ISOBELL, children of **James M**, mason in Aberdeen, 12 Oct 1732.
MACKIE, JOHN, portioner in Inverury, see **Elizabeth Anderson.**
MACKIE, PATRICK, in Clunymoir, 27 Jul 1727.
MACKIE, WILLIAM, Mr, late chamberlain of Balquhine, 14 Jun 1727.
MAIR, MARY, in Millseat, 20 Jul 1723.
MAIR, ROBERT, in Broadford of Towie, 21 Feb 1734.
MAITLAND, ALEXANDER, lawful son of the late **Richard M**, in Lewes of Fyvie, 11 Dec 1724.
MAITLAND, ALEXANDER, Mr, of Pitrichie, one of the Barons of HM Exchequer in Scotland, 11 Aug 1726.
MAITLAND, JOHN, Mr, late minister at Banchory Devnick, 31 Jul 1727.
MALICE, GEORGE, of Tillieangus, 4 Jun 1730.
MAN, JOHN, tidewaiter in Aberdeen, 20 Mar 1723.
MARISCHALL, ROBERT, in Over Deuchry, 28 Feb 1724.
MARK, GEORGE, sometime at Craigilly, and **Elizabeth Wood**, his wife, 22 Jan 1734.
MARK, JOHN, merchant, and late provost of Banff, 13 Jul 1732.
MARK, WILLIAM, merchant in Craigs, 13 Jan 1724.
MASSON, JANET, in Baley, 15 Aug 1728.
MEARNS, JAMES, merchant in Inch, 23 Jun 1734.
MEARNS, ROBERT, chapman in Aberdeen, 24 Aug 1726.
MEARNS, WILLIAM, merchant in Inch of Garrioch, 20 Oct 1732.
MELVILL, CHRISTIAN, wife of **Gilbert Thomson**, in Clovenstone, and her said husband, 10 Aug 1722.
MELVILL, FRANCIS, Mr, one of the ministers of Aberdeen, 20 Feb 1724. See also **Margaret Turnbull.**
MELVILL, GILBERT, Mr, in Hardgate of Aberdeen, sometime minister at Glenduan, 3 Feb 1732.
MELVILL, KATHARINE, Mrs, Lady Dowager of Echt, 22 Jan 1730.
MELVILL, THOMAS, in Woodside, 10 Dec 1721.
MELVILL, WLATER, merchant in Aberdeen, 27 Apr 1727.

MENZIES, ANNE, Mrs, daughter of the late **Gilbert M** of Pitfoddles, 20 Jun 1727.

MENZIES, PAULL, dyer in Aberdeen, 24 May 1722.

MENZIES, ROBERT, at Miln of Gilkomstone, see **Jean Wauchop**.

MERCER, JAMES, merchant in Aberdeen, see **Anne Irvine**.

MERCHANT, ROBERT, sometime in Wartle, thereafter in Oldtoun of Auchlossen, 4 Feb 1732.

MICHIE, JOHN, in Glencarvie, 11 Feb 1726.

MIDDLETON, ELIZABETH, schoolmistress at Banchory, 26 Nov 1724.

MIDDLETON, JOHN, gardener in Fetterneir, 23 Feb 1732.

MIDDLETON, SAMUEL, in Tillyharmick, 17 Feb 1725.

MIDDLETON, WILLIAM, in Muirtoun, 13 Nov 1730.

MILLER, JANET, widow of **James Allan**, merchant in Aberdeen, 6 Feb 1728.

MILNE, ALEXANDER, town-clerk depute of Aberdeen, and **Isobell Moir**, his wife, 9 Apr 1729 and 19 Jun 1734.

MITCHELL, ALEXANDER, Mr, writer in Aberdeen, 13 Aug 1722 and 13 Aug 1723.

MITCHELL, ALEXANDER, in Cairntoun, 18 Jun 1724.

MITCHELL, ALEXANDER, of Colpnay, minister at Old Machar, 8 Feb 1728.

MITCHELL, WILLIAM, in Camalegie, 2 Mar 1722.

MOIR, ALEXANDER, in Tirrefield, 15 Dec 1731.

MOIR, ANDREW, at Oldmill of Foverane, 6 Nov (Dec) 1733.

MOIR, ISOBELL, see **Alexander Milne**.

MOIR, JAMES, mariner in Aberdeen, 16 Feb 1722.

MOIR, WILLIAM, alias **Cuming** in Ballachbuie, 17 Jan 1727.

MORGAN, WILLIAM, sometime in Easter Tulloch, thereafter in Breas of Bullogie, 27 Jan 1726.

MORISON, CHRISTIAN, widow of William Troup, merchant in Aberdeen, 13 Jun 1734.

MORTIMER, JAMES, sometime in Ardgathen, 15 Mar 1726.

MORTIMER, ROBERT, merchant in Banff, 22 Feb 1723.

MORTIMER, WILLIAM, late of Glencale, 25 May 1733.

MOWAT, JAMES, in Cookstoune, 18 Jul 1724.

MOWAT, MAGNUS, in Milltoun of Finan, 7 Feb 1723.

MOWAT, WILLIAM, of Balquholly, 8 Nov 1728.

MUIRISON, ANDREW, servant to Earl of Kintore, 17 Dec 1729.

MUIRISON, JAMES, in Cairngall, 22 Oct 1726.

MULLIGAN, JOHN, Mr, minister at Methlick, 31 Jul 1733. See also **Isobell Udny**.

MURRAY, GEORGE, sometime wigmaker in Old Aberdeen, and **John M**, his son, 15 Apr 1725.

MURRAY, JOHN, in Greenyeards of Balrouny, etc, see **Jean Wemyss**.

MURRAY, THOMAS, town-clerk of Cullen, 4 Jan 1733.

NICOL, AGNES, see **Alexander Fyfe**.

NICOL, ELSPET, widow of **John Airth**, sometime in Brousterbog, 5 Jan 1725.

NICOL, ELSPET, in Bankhead, 5 Dec 1734.

NICOL, JAMES, wigmaker in Aberdeen, 3 Aug 1727 (18 Mar 1728).

NOBLE, GILBERT, tidewaiter in Aberdeen, see **Mary Jaffray**.

OGILVIE, ALEXANDER, shipmaster in Banff, 12 Feb 1729.

OGILVIE, ALEXANDER, in Gateside of Kinisky, 16 Oct 1733.

OGILVIE, ANNA, widow of **Alexander Hay**, late burgess of Cullen, 2 Jul 1734.

OGILVIE, GEORGE, of Forglan, 11 Mar 1724.

OGILVIE, JAMES, in Toux, 15 May 1731.

OGILVIE, JEAN, sometime wife to **Alexander Shewan**, in Millhill, parish of Monymusk, 18 Sep 1733.

OGILVIE, PATRICK, sometime of Raggle, 17 Jan 1732. See also **Elizabeth Dunbar**.

OGILVIE, THOMAS, dyer in Banff, 19 Sep 1733.

OGILVIE, WALTER, in Fintre, see **Elspet Ronald**.

OGSTON, JAMES, merchant in Peterhead, 10 Mar 1729.

ORD, HELEN, widow of **William Baird**, late bailie of Cullen, 11 Mar 1726.

ORD, WILLIAM, Mr, merchant in Deskford, 3 Apr 1733.

OREM, ALEXANDER, late bailie and merchant in Aberdeen, 17 Feb 1722, 16 Feb 1726 and 12 Mar 1729.

OREM, JEAN, wife to Mr **Francis Downie**, tenant in Mains of Kemnay, 16 Feb 1727.

OREM, JOHN, late in Badiefurrow, thereafter in Blairdaff, 3 Jul 1723.

OSBURN, WILLIAM, Mr, minister at Fintray, 1 Feb 1733.

PAIP, THOMAS, Mr, servitor to Sir Alexander Cuming, of Culter, eldest son of the late **Thomas P**, merchant in Aberdeen, 9 Aug 1722.

PANTON, JOHN, in Holls of Culfurnie, 9 Jun 1732.

PANTON, WILLIAM, in Milntoun of Fyvie, 5 Apr 1727.

PANTON, WILLIAM, in Delgatie, 3 Oct 1734.

PARK, JAMES, at Mill of Rora, 29 Sep 1732.

PATERSON, ALEXANDER, armorer, burgess of Aberdeen, see **Janet Baird**.

PATERSON, JEAN, daughter to late **Thomas P**, sometime in Todlachie of Monymusk, 1 Aug 1727.

PATERSON, JOHN, in Clubcroft, 24 Feb 1730.

PATERSON, ROBERT, in Swidly, 14 Jan 1724.

PATERSON, ROBERT, Mr, late commissary of Aberdeen, 3 Jul 1729.

PATON, ALEXANDER, in Kinnaldy, late provost of Aberdeen, 10 Aug 1724.

PAUL, ISOBELL, wife to **Andrew Littlejohn**, in Midletoun of Blackfoord, 23 Oct 1728.

PEDDER, JANET, daughter to **Thomas P**, in Old Deer, 22 Jul 1726.

PEDDER, JOHN, writer in Aberdeen, 30 Nov 1721.

PENNY, WILLIAM, in Midleton, 15 Jul 1729.

PETRIE, JAMES, in Blachrie, 18 Oct 1723.

PHANS, WILLIAM, late convener of the Trades of Aberdeen, 7 Jun 1733.

PHILP, AGNES, widow of **John Kemp**, sometime in Brea of Balogie, 15 Jun 1731.

PRATT, JOHN, shipmaster in Aberdeen, 21 Aug 1724.

PYPER, GILBERT, feuar in Turriff, 16 Feb 1733.

RAE, PETER, in Bogend, 13 Jan 1731.

RAIT, JOHN, tailor in Aberdeen, 8 Feb 1728.

RAMSAY, GILBERT, Mr, late minister at Dyce, 24 Jun 1728.

RATTRAY, THOMAS, merchant in Aberdeen, 9 Oct 1731.

RAWER, JOHN, in Drumnethy, 10 Jun 1729.

REID, ALEXANDER, in Cutlebrae, 28 Feb 1722.

REID, ALEXANDER, tailor, burgess in Aberdeen, see **Margaret Grant**.

REID, ALEXANDER, of Glassell, 14 Nov 1726.

REID, ELSPET, widow of **Peter Forbes**, in Dunideer, 11 Jun 1724.

REID, JOHN, in Gownie, 5 Aug 1724.

REID, JOHN, Mr, minister of Dyce, 2 Apr 1728.

REID, THOMAS, see **Jean Burnet**.

REITH, ANDREW, in Collonoch, 21 Apr 1727.

REITH, JOHN, Chamberlain to the Earl of Aberdeen, 27 Jul 1725.

RICKART, DAVID, of Rickartoun, 20 Sep 1718. See also Mrs **Katharine Arbuthnot**.

RIDLER, JANET, wife of **Alexander Burnet**, in Upper Banchory, 7 Aug 1733.

RITCHIE, ANDREW, of Forresterhill, merchant in Aberdeen, 25 Jul 1722.

RITCHIE, JOHN, sometime in Lews of Fyvie, 31 Jul 1729.

RITCHIE, WILLIAM, in Brainly, 25 Jun 1724.

ROBERTSON, ADAM, at Milne of Balmade, 20 Jul 1726.

ROBERTSON, ALEXANDER, in Cairnhall, 10 Aug 1722.

ROBERTSON, ALEXANDER, tailor in Aberdeen, 4 Jun 1734.

ROBERTSON, ALEXANDER, see **John Robertson**.

ROBERTSON, CHARLES, see **Elspet Robertson**.

ROBERTSON, ELSPET, lawful daughter to the late **Charles R**, at Mill of Bellamore, 24 Apr 1733.

ROBERTSON, JAMES, late bailie in Aberdeen, 4 Jun 1730.

ROBERTSON, JOHN, son of **Alexander R**, in Midbeattie, 17 Apr 1732.

ROBERTSON, JOHN, Mr, sometime minister at Finnylost, thereafter at Whitehouse of Cromar, 25 Jul 1734.

ROBERTSON, THOMAS, in Mains of Castle Fraser, 17 Mar 1724.

ROLLAND, ELIZABETH, Mrs, eldest lawful daughter to the late **James R**, younger, of Disblair, 26 Oct 1733.

RONALD, ELSPET, widow of **Walter Ogilvie**, of Fintray, 14 Mar 1723.

RONALDSON, ANDREW, see **William Ronaldson**.

RONALDSON, GEORGE, see **William Ronaldson**.

RONALDSON, JOHN, see **William Ronaldson**.

RONALDSON, WILLIAM, in Wester Cairnie, JOHN, ANDREW, and GEORGE R, his children, 12 Feb 1729.

ROSS, ALEXANDER, Mr, minister at Auchterless, 22 Feb 1731.

ROSS, ANDREW, of Balblair, see **Margaret Gellie**.

ROSS, ARTHUR, son of **John R**, of Arnadge, late Provost of Aberdeen, 3 Jun 1724.

ROSS, ELIZABETH, widow of **Duncan Sivewright** of Drummachie, 3 Feb 1729.

ROSS, GEORGE, peutherer in Aberdeen, 28 Feb 1724.

ROSS, HUGH, peutherer, burgess of Aberdeen, 15 Nov 1723.

ROSS, JAMES, in Braehead of Mortlich, 17 Oct 1724.

ROSS, JAMES, in Balgreen, 19 Feb 1730.

ROSS, JAMES, late servant to James, Earl of Finlater and Seafield, 19 Nov 1731.

ROSS, JEAN, resident in Aberdeen, 25 Sep 1729.

ROSS, JOHN, of Arnadge, late provost of Aberdeen, 12 Feb 1715.

ROSS, JOHN, see **Arthur Ross**.

ROSS, MARGARET, wife to **Robert Gellan**, late butcher, burgess of Aberdeen, 24 Feb 1726.

ROSS, MARJORY, widow of **James Catanach**, sometime in Belnabodach, 17 Jun 1731.

ROSS, THOMAS, in Old Meldrum, 13 Feb 1724.

ROY, JOHN, merchant in Craigincatt, 9 Oct 1723.

RUSSELL, ALEXANDER, of Montcoffer, 13 Jun 1732.

SANDILANDS, JEAN, widow of **Robert Byres**, merchant in Dublin, 4 Aug 1730.

SANDILANDS, JOHN, of Countesswells, late provost of Aberdeen, 8 Nov 1723.

SANDILANDS, JOHN, of Countesswells, late provost of Aberdeen, and **John S**, younger, his son, 26 Jan 1726.

SANDILANDS, ROBERT, merchant in Aberdeen, son of the late Mr **James S**, of Craibston, 18 Dec 1724.

SANGSTER, GILBERT, mason in Aberdeen, 26 May 1730.

SANGSTER, JOHN, in Lochtoun of Keithfield, 20 Feb 1733.

SCOTT, GEORGE, Mr, town clerk of Inverurie, 6 Jun 1732.

SCOTT, JAMES, of Auchtidonald, 10 Jul 1722.

SCOTT, JOHN, in Peterwell, 16 Aug 1729.

SCOTT, THOMAS, barber, burgess of Aberdeen, see **Mary Innes**.

SCOUGALL, MARGARET, widow of Mr **Patrick Harvie**, of Mamevlaw, late minister at Forgue, 28 Dec 1722.

SELBIE, PATRICK, in Graystone, 26 Jun 1730.

SELLER, ALEXANDER, shipmaster in Aberdeen, 1 Sep 1731.

SETON, JAMES, sometime at Mill of Gilkomstone, thereafter at Oldrain, see **Jean Gow**.

SETON, JANET, widow of Mr **Robert Harvie**, of Mamevlaw, 29 Jan 1724.

SHAND, PATRICK, merchant in Aberdeen, 16 Mar 1720, 5 Dec 1754, and 20 Mar 1749, see also **Isobell Legertwood**.

SHEARER, WILLIAM, merchant in Tynet, in the parish of Ruthven, 4 Aug 1731.

SHEPHERD, GEORGE, in Midskeith, 23 Mar 1726.

SHEPHERD, GEORGE, tailor, burgess of Aberdeen, see **Isabell Gordon**.

SHEWAN, ALEXANDER, in Millhill, parish of Monymusk, see **Jean Ogilvie**.

SHIRRAS, ALEXANDER, in Drumnagourthe, 30 Jul 1734.

SHIRRAS, WILLIAM, merchant in Aberdeen, 24 Oct 1734.

SHORT, JAMES, apprentice to James Shand, cooper in Aberdeen, 7 Jun 1727.

SIBALD, DAVID, see **Elizabeth Sibald**.

SIBALD, ELIZABETH, widow of Mr **David S**, minister at Auchredy, 25 Apr 1722.

SILLIE, JOHN, gardener at the King's College of Aberdeen, 28 Nov 1732.

SIMPSON, GEORGE, merchant in Aberdeen, 24 Oct 1727 and 9 Sep 1734.

SIMPSON, GEORGE, see **John Simpson**.

SIMPSON, JOHN, merchant in Old Meldrum, and **George S**, merchant there, 20 Mar 1725.

SIMPSON, JOHN, merchant in Old Meldrum, 24 Feb 1732.

SIMPSON, THOMAS, merchant in Old Meldrum, 17 Sep 1729 and 4 Sep 1733.

SINCLAIR, JAMES, sometime schoolmaster at Deskford, 15 Apr 1730.

SIVENTON, JOHN, merchant in Petertoun, 28 Apr 1732.

SIVEWRIGHT, DUNCAN, of Druminachie, see **Elizabeth Ross**.

SKENE, ALEXANDER, of that Ilk, 25 Jan 1726.

SKENE, BARBARA, wife to **John Tytler**, in Cursenday, 1 Jun 1731.

SKENE, CHRISTIAN, widow of **George Gordon**, merchant in Aberdeen, 3 Feb 1726.

SKENE, GEORGE, Mr, minister at Kinkell, 11 Aug 1724 and 25 Apr 1728.

SKENE, WILLIAM, in Tillieludge, 16 Oct 1730.

SKINNER, JAMES, sometime in Leachie, 3 Jan 1724.

SKLAIT, GILBERT, in Hill of Crimond, 4 Jun (Jul) 1728.

SMART, JAMES, sometime in Miln of Williamstone, 3 May 1728, see also **Jean Wilson**.

SMART, JEAN, widow of **John Allardice**, late provost of Aberdeen, 20 Jun 1723 and 3 Jun 1729.

SMITH, ALEXANDER, at Mill of Rothie, 19 Jul 1723.

SMITH, ALEXANDER, in Belskevie, and **Alexander S**, his son, 27 Jan 1726.

SMITH, ALEXANDER, lawful son of the late **James S**, in Quartans, 1 Mar 1734.

SMITH, ANDREW, merchant in Old Aberdeen, 1 Jul 1724.

SMITH, ANDREW, in Overside of St Fergus, 23 Mar 1730.

SMITH, CHRISTIAN, widow of **Patrick Forbes**, shipmaster in Aberdeen, 4 Apr 1726.

SMITH, GEORGE, notary public in Old Meldrum, 4 Sep 1733.

SMITH, GEORGE, feuar in Fraserburgh, and **Isobell Bisset**, his wife, 10 Aug 1734.

SMITH, JAMES, in Overside of St Fergus, 10 Feb 1732.

SMITH, JAMES, gunsmith in Aberdeen, see **Jean Johnston**.

SMITH, JAMES, see **Alexander Smith**.

SMITH, JANET, lawful daughter to the late **William S**, late bailie of Peterhead, 7 Feb 1733.

SMITH, JANET, widow of **John Ferguson**, sometime in Kirkhill, 21 May 1733.

SMITH, JOHN, in Cairnglass, 18 Jun 1731.

SMITH, JOHN, messenger in Aberdeen, 28 Aug 1732 and 17 Dec 1733.

SMITH, MARGARET, widow of **James Edward**, in Letter of Skene, 25 May 1732.

SMITH, PETER, in Mostoun of Blelack, 28 Sep 1725.

SMITH, ROBERT, in Hillhead of Lethinty, 6 Jun 1727.

SMITH, ROBERT, merchant in Peterhead, see **Jean Fraser**.

SMITH, WILLIAM, Mr, minister at Old Aberdeen, 1 Mar 1734.

SMITH, WILLIAM, see **Janet Smith**.
SPENCE, JAMES, and Mr **James**, in Pennyburn, 25 Jan 1722.
SPENCE, LODOVICK, mariner in Aberdeen, 12 Oct 1724.
SPRING, GEORGE, weaver in Hillocks of Auchinhive, 8 Mar 1726.
STEILL, ANDREW, sometime seaman in Burghsea, thereafter in the
    parish of Raffen, 3 Sep 1728.
STEPHEN, GEORGE, in Sweltoun, and **Isobel Black**, his wife, 1 Nov
    1723.
STEPHEN, ISOBELL, widow of **Alexander Ferguson**, farmer in Old
    Aberdeen, 18 Nov 1731.
STEPHEN, JOHN, sometime in Auchlyne, 28 Nov 1723.
STEPHEN, THOMAS, in Easterbeltie, see **Margaret Couts**.
STEPHEN, WILLIAM, in Inverury, 13 Feb 1722.
STEVENSON, ELSPET, in Cullen, 31 May 1722.
STEWART, ALEXANDER, of Lesmurdie, 6 Jun 1728.
STEWART, CHARLES, in Starbridge, 11 Jul 1727.
STEWART, GEORGE, of Boggs, sometime designed of Rosieburn, 18
    Jan 1732.
STEWART, GEORGE, junior, merchant, and sometime bailie in Banff, 19
    Dec 1734.
STEWART, HELEN, in Knowhead, see **William Gibbon**.
STEWART, JAMES, in Hillend, 26 Mar 1724.
STEWART, JOHN, Capt, of Denns, and **Agnes Gray**, his spouse, 11 Dec
    1729.
STEWART, ROBERT, in Milntoun of Lesmurdie, 6 Jun 1728.
STEWART, WILLIAM, of Auchoillie, 7 Nov 1729.
STILL, JAMES, merchant, burgess of Aberdeen, 30 Jul 1723.
STONE, JOHN, shipmaster in Fraserburgh, 28 Feb 1732.
STRACHAN, ALEXANDER, brother-german to Sir **Patrick S**, of
    Glenkindy, 7 Jul 1732.
STRACHAN, MARGARET, see **James Gordon**.
STRACHAN, PATRICK, Sir, of Glenkindie, see **Alexander Strachan**.
STRACHAN, PATRICK, sometime servant to Glenkindy, 5 Feb 1730.
STRACHAN, ROBERT, Mr, of Tillieriach, 7 Sep 1725, 13 Jan 1727 and
    11 Feb 1732. See also **Marjory Garrioch**.
STRACHAN, THOMAS, in Brae of Biffie, 26 Jan 1722.
STRACHAN, WILLIAM, shoemaker in Banff, see **Isobell Cock**.
SUTHERLAND, ADAM, Mr, late parson of Duffus, see **Elizabeth Dun**.
SUTOR, ALEXANDER, in Wester Clava, 1 Aug 1728.
SWAP, PATRICK, merchant in Aberdeen, 20 Mar 1722.
SYME, THOMAS, cooper, burgess of Aberdeen, 17 Mar 1726.
TAWS, JOHN, sometime in Ordie, 12 Jun 1733.

TAYLOR, AGNES, widow of **James Aberdeen**, in Bailliestoun of Dyce, 7 Jul 1727.

TAYLOR, ALEXANDER, in Newparks, 13 Mar 1725.

TAYLOR, WILLIAM, merchant in Aberdeen, 20 Sep 1723. See also **Margaret Gray**.

TAYLOR, WILLIAM, in Hillhead, 17 Jul 1727.

TERSIE, GEORGE, merchant in Old Meldrum, 24 Feb 1733.

THAIN, JOHN, of Blackhall, 2 Mar 1724.

THOMSON, ANDREW, see **William Thomson**.

THOMSON, CHRISTIAN, see **Gilbert Davidson**.

THOMSON, GILBERT, in Clovenstone, see **Christian Melvill**.

THOMSON, JOHN, sometime servant to Mr Alexander Rose, of Lethinty, 18 Sep 1724.

THOMSON, JOHN, in Bagrymilns, 21 Nov 1727.

THOMSON, THOMAS, of Faichfield, 15 Oct 1723 and 22 Aug 1724.

THOMSON, WILLIAM, son of **Andrew T**, advocate in Aberdeen, 17 Dec 1728.

THOMSON, WILLIAM, Mr, late minister at Peterculter, 22 Oct 1731 (1730).

TOWER, ROBERT, junior, merchant in Aberdeen, 29 Oct 1723.

TROUP, GEORGE, in Ashenhead, 25 Feb 1725.

TROUP, WILLIAM, merchant in Aberdeen, 16 Dec 1731 and 5 Apr 1733, see **Christian Morison**.

TURNBULL, MARGARET, widow of Mr Francis Melvill, one of the ministers of Aberdeen, 10 Jul 1725.

TYTLER, JOHN, in Cursenday, see **Barbara Skene**.

URQUHART, JAMES, merchant and late bailie in Fraserburgh, 7 Dec 1730.

WALKER, BARBARA, wife to **John Deuchar**, at Mill of Garlogie, 18 Feb 1731.

WALKER, GEORGE, farmer in Seaton, 30 Jun 1722.

WALKER, GEORGE, merchant in Aberdeen, 31 Aug 1732.

WALKER, JAMES, Mr, in Kinmuck, 1 Aug 1722.

WALKER, JOHN, goldsmith in Aberdeen, 26 Jan 1728.

WATSON, JAMES, cooper in Aberdeen, 22 Jun 1724.

WATSON, JANET, sometime in Rora, 26 Sep 1733.

WATSON, JOHN, merchant in Aberdeen, 9 Nov 1724.

WATSON, JOHN, wright, burgess of Aberdeen, 12 Jan 1725.

WAUCHOP, JEAN, widow of **Robert Menzies**, at Miln of Gilkomstone, 8 Aug 1730.

WEBSTER, ALEXANDER, in Pitgevnie, 20 Jul and 31 Dec 1724.

WEMYSS, JEAN, widow of **John Murray**, sometime in Greenyeards of Balrouny, in the parish of Menmuir, late in Ardmenach, in the parish of Inamuick, 27 Feb 1729.

WEMYSS, JOHN, in Aberdour, see **Jean Forbes**.

WHITE, PATRICK, convenor of the Trades of Aberdeen, thereafter resident in Old Aberdeen, 21 Feb 1724.

WHITE, WILLIAM, of Heivmill of Auchterless, 7 Jan 1723.

WILLIAMSON, ALEXANDER, merchant in Hattown of Fintray, 30 Dec 1734.

WILLIAMSON, KATHARINE, sometime wife to **George Duff**, of Stockbrigg, 17 Apr 1724.

WILSON, GEORGE, of Finzeach, 4 Oct 1725 and 13 Feb 1728.

WILSON, JAMES, in Torries of Touch, and **Christian Elmsie**, his wife, 11 Jun 1724.

WILSON, LEWES, sometime in Formestoun, 6 Nov 1724.

WILSON, WILLIAM, in Bowstocks, 8 Feb 1723.

WILSON, WILLIAM, in Meithlick, 24 Oct 1723.

WINCHESTER, ISAAC, schoolmaster in Kinmuck, 7 Nov 1722.

WISEMAN, ALEXANDER, sometime maltman in Cullen, 1 Nov 1726.

WISHART, ELIZABETH, resident and late servitrix to Mrs Menzies in Aberdeen, 13 Nov 1730.

WISHART, JOHN, sometime in Old Meldrum, see **Janet Ferguson**.

WOOD, ELIZABETH, see **George Mark**.

WOODROPE, WILLIAM, sometime merchant in Glasgow, land surveyor of HM Customs at Aberdeen, 15 Feb 1731.

REGISTER OF TESTAMENTS
ABERDEEN

Part Two: 1735-1759

INTRODUCTION

Some of the most important sources of information on our ancestors are to be found in the form of testaments. These documents can be expected to reveal the name and designation of the deceased, normally the date of death, the executor, an inventory of assets, liabilities, debtors and creditors, and usually a will. Registers of Testaments are generally available from the late 16th century to the early 19th century, and these contain significant material of relevance to the family historian. It should, however, be noted that not everyone left a will, and of those made, not all found their way into the books of the Commissary Court.

Until the 1820s, testaments in Scotland were "confirmed", by various Commissariot Courts throughout the land. These Courts were based roughly on pre-Reformation dioceses boundaries. The Commissariot Court of Edinburgh was often used by Scots residing overseas. After the 1820s, documents were usually, but not exclusively, lodged in the local Sheriff Court, with Edinburgh continuing to be used by those living abroad.

Fire destroyed the early records of the Commisariot of Aberdeen, including testaments, and the surviving records date only from 1715. This publication is in essence an alphabetical listing of the testaments confirmed by the Commissary Court of Aberdeen for the period 1735 to 1759.

The documents relating to those listed in this booklet can be viewed at the Scottish Record Office, Edinburgh.

St Andrews
1997

REGISTER OF TESTAMENTS
ABERDEEN
1735-1759

ABERCROMBIE, ALEXANDER, Capt, of Glassaugh, 22 Jan and 25 Apr 1730, 15 Aug 1732, 2 Feb 1738, 10 Jun 1741.

ABERCROMBIE, JOHN, in Leys of Cromar, 24 May 1736.

ABERCROMBIE, JOHN, excise officer in Turriff, 11 Dec 1739.

ABERCROMBIE, ROBERT, Mr, late minister at Leslie, 21 Dec 1751.

ABERCROMBIE, WILLIAM, Mr, minister at Skene, 23 Dec 1747.

ABERDEEN, WILLIAM, merchant in Old Aberdeen, 20 Mar 1749.

ABERNETHY, ELIZABETH, widow of Mr **Hugh Innes**, sometime minister at Mortlack, 31 Oct 1752.

ABERNETHY, JEAN, widow of **James More**, of Stonywood, 19 Dec 1749.

ACHYNACHY, ALEXANDER, of Kincraigiem, sometime chamberlain of Fyvie, 18 Jun 1740.

ACHYNACHY, GEORGE, OF Kincraigie, 8 May 1742.

ADAM, JOHN, in Arnadlie of Monymusk, 26 Feb 1752.

ADAMSON, CHRISTIAN, wife of **David Speediman**, glover; burgess of Aberdeen, 27 Oct 1756.

ADAMSON, JAMES, Mr, minister at Ordiequhill, 8 Jun 1757.

ADIE, ELSPETH, in Crofts of Achlyne, 23 Apr 1742.

ADIE, GILES, widow of **Alexander Skene**, of that Ilk, 31 Dec 1751.

ADIELL, WILLIAM, in Nether-Brownhill, 4 Sep 1739.

AIRTH, JOHN, merchant in Peterhead, 9 Mar 1751.

AITKINE, JOHN, in Druminachie, 17 Dec 1750.

ALEXANDER, ALEXANDER, at Kirk of Forgue, 12 May 1738.

ALEXANDER, GEORGE, mariner in Aberdeen, 4 Feb 1755.

ALEXANDER, GILBERT, tailor in Peterhead, 6 Apr 1756.

ALEXANDER, JANET, widow of **John Ross**, sometime merchant in Aberdeen, 12 May 1737.

ALEXANDER, JAMES, mason in Aberdeen, see **Marjory Davidson**.

ALEXANDER, JOHN, Mr, sometime minister at Kildrimmy, 24 Jul 1738.

ALEXANDER, MARGARET, at Leslie, 26 Apr 1745.

ALLAN, JOHN, sometime maltman in Pitsligo, 29 Jul 1735.

ALLAN, JOHN, sometime in Dorsinsilly, see **Elspeth Elmsly**.

ALLAN, SUSAN, in Mackterry, widow of **James Mutch**, sometime in Kingsfoord, 26 Mar 1754.

ALLARDICE, JAMES, merchant in Aberdeen, 13 Nov 1736.

ALLARDICE, MARGARET, in Nether Boddom, 22 May 1748.

ALLASTER, ALEXANDER, in Guise of Findlater, 27 Jun 1739.

ANDERSON, ALEXANDER, in Balnagald, thereafter in Kandacraig, 29 Jan 1736.

ANDERSON, AGNES and ELIZABETH, daughters of the late **John A**, writer in Aberdeen, 7 Dec 1749.

ANDERSON, ALEXANDER, see **Rachel Anderson**.

ANDERSON, ANDREW, in Milne of Boyndlie, 15 Apr 1742.   See **Thomas Anderson**.

ANDERSON, ANNA, widow of **Francis Grant** of Touchar, 20 Dec 1754.

ANDERSON, ELIZABETH, see **William Ingram**.

ANDERSON, ELIZABETH, see **Agnes Anderson**.

ANDERSON, GILBERT, merchant in Aberdeen, 30 Jan 1749.

ANDERSON, ISOBELL, wife of **John Durno**, in Mill of Barns, 3 Jan 1739.

ANDERSON, JAMES, Mr, minister at Raithen, 19 Feb 1741.

ANDERSON, JEAN, see **James Torn**.

ANDERSON, JOHN, dyer, burgess in Old Aberdeen, 30 Mar 1742.

ANDERSON, JOHN, dyer in Old Meldrum, 29 Apr 1743.

ANDERSON, JOHN, master of English School of Aberdeen, 31 Jul 1744.

ANDERSON, MARGARET, widow of **George Sangster**, tanner in Old Aberdeen, 18 Feb 1743.

ANDERSON, MARGARET, widow of **John Watt**, in Bridgend of Logiedurno, 8 May 1746.

ANDERSON, RACHEL, daughter of late **Alexander A**, sometime of Bourtie, 29 Nov 1753.

ANDERSON, THOMAS, sometime writer in Edinburgh, son of late **Andrew A**, sometime at Mill of Boyndlie, 20 Sep 1743.

ANDERSON, WILLIAM, Mr, minister at Daviot, 5 Oct 1742.

ANNAND, JANET, in Old Aberdeen, 13 Dec 1744.

ANNAND, WILLIAM, in Smiddyhill of Slains, 19 Apr 1753.

ANNAND, WILLIAM, in Bogsheads of Kinmundy, 28 Oct 1736.

ARBUTHNOT, ALEXANDER, dyer in Peterhead, 2 Nov 1742.

ARBUTHNOT, JAMES, shipmaster in Peterhead, 2 Nov 1742.

ARBUTHNOT, KATHARINE, Mrs, widow of **David Rickart**, of Rickartoun, 9 Sep 1746.

ARBUTHNOT, KATHARINE, Mrs, wife of **Thomas Mercer**, merchant in Aberdeen, 3 Jul 1749.

ARBUTHNOT, MARGARET, Dame, widow of Sir **Thomas Burnet**, of Leys, 23 Jan 1745.

ARBUTHNOT, MAY, Mrs, see Mr **William Dunbar**.

ARCHIBALD, ALEXANDER, in Murthill, 21 Mar 1739.

ARCHIBALD, WILLIAM, in Mill of Clatt, 25 May 1739.

ARTHUR, WILLIAM, wright in Aberdeen, 15 Aug 1752.

BADENOCH, WILLIAM, Mr, minister at Alford, 23 Jun 1747.

BAIN, ALEXANDER, husband to **Jean Thomson**, in Milntoun of Kemnay, 6 Jun 1744.

BAIN, WILLIAM, in Mill of Hole, 18 Feb 1752.

BAIRD, JAMES, Bailie, merchant in Auchmeden, 27 Feb 1736.

BAIRD, MARGARET, widow of Dr **James Gordon**, younger of Fechill, 7 Sep 1742.

BAILLIE, ALEXANDER, wright, burgess of Aberdeen, 8 Oct 1740.

BALFOUR, WILLIAM, sometime surgeon at Quartale-house, 5 Jan 1747.

BANFF, HELEN, Lady, 30 Jun 1743.

BANFF, JOHN GEORGE, Lord, 28 Feb 1739.

BANNERMAN, ALEXANDER, town sergeant of Aberdeen, see **Jean Laurence**.

BANNERMAN, PATRICK, of Frendraught, merchant in Aberdeen, 29 Sep 1736.

BARCLAY, ADAM, Mr, and CHARLES, lawful sons of the late Mr **Adam B**, sometime minister at Perth, 10 Jun 1735.

BARCLAY, BARBARA, lawful daughter to the late Mr **Adam B**, sometime minister at Perth and widow of the late Mr **William Mair**, minister at Kincardine O'Neill, 10 Jun 1735.

BARCLAY, CHARLES, see **Adam Barclay**.

BARCLAY, LEWIS, late of Inverchat, 25 Jul 1757 and 5 Dec 1758.

BARCLAY, PATRICK, at Mill of Towie, 9 Jul 1757.

BARNET, AGNES, widow of **John Gibson**, in Nether Leask, 20 Feb 1752.

BARNET, ELSPETH, resident of Aberdeen, 3 Jun 1756.

BARRON, CHRISTIAN, daughter of the late **Patrick B** in Poddockhall, and wife of **John Glenny**, in Mains of Strathlock, 20 May 1736.

BARRON, PATRICK, see **Christian Barron**.

BARSKINE, JAMES, in the parish of Newhills, 26 Jun 1739.

BARTLET, JAMES, merchant in Old Aberdeen, 20 Mar 1751 and 29 Jul 1752.

BARTLET, WILLIAM, tenant in Kinmundy, 29 Nov 1749.

BAXTER, ALEXANDER, of Glassell, 22 May 1758.

BAXTER, JAMES, son of Adam B, cooper in Aberdeen, 7 Apr 1755.

BAXTER, THOMAS, in Auchinleith, 16 Oct 1736.

BEATTIE, WILLIAM, in Baads, 15 Aug 1754.

BEGG, JAMES, in Tomnavoan, parish of Tullich, 24 Jul 1750.

BEGG, THOMAS, late in Meikle Tipperty, 20 Jul 1758.

BEVERLY, GEORGE, late bailie in Inverury, 17 Apr 1747.

BEVERLY, JAMES, lately in Lochills, thereafter in Old Aberdeen, 14 Oct 1748 and 27 Dec 1750. See also **Isobell Still.**

BIRNIE, ANDREW, sailor in Peterhead, 12 Jun 1753.

BIRNIE, JAMES, at Mill of Boindly, 18 Jun 1745.

BIRSS, JOHN, in Craigton of Midleton of Kincardine, 12 Dec 1752.

BISSET, ALEXANDER, tailor in Selbie, parish of Keithhall, 4 Nov 1748.

BISSET, CHARLES, brother-german to late **Robert B** of Lessendrum, 16 Sep 1742 and 14 Apr 1744.

BISSET, GEORGE, brother-german to late **Robert B** of Lessendrum, 14 Apr 1744.

BISSET, JAMES, of Lessendrum, 18 Jun 1747.

BISSET, JEAN, daughter of the late James B, of Lessendrum, 22 Aug 1757.

BISSET, JOHN, Mr, late minister at Aberdeen, 28 Jun 1757.

BISSET, ROBERT, see **Charles** and **George Bisset.**

BLACK, AGNES, late resident in Aberdeen, 11 Jun 1752.

BLACK, JAMES, merchant and late baillie of Aberdeen, 10 Mar 1756.

BLACK, JOHN, in Damadilly, 20 Jun 1758.

BLACK, PATRICK, of Haddo, 29 Jul 1745 and 20 Dec 1746.

BLACKWELL, THOMAS, Mr, principal of the Marischall College of Aberdeen, 30 May 1728, 9 May 1757, and 31 Jan 1758.

BLYTH, JAMES, merchant in Old Meldrum, 7 Oct 1747.

BOGG, CHARLES, Mr, preacher at Corriehoul, parish of Strathdon, 24 Jul 1759.

BOGIE, ANNA, in Corsindae, 27 Nov 1744.

BONNAR, WILLIAM, in Milnhill, parish of Tillinesee, and **Janet Forbes**, his wife, 19 Jul 1750.

BOOTH, ALEXANDER, merchant in Aberdeen, and **Rachel Nithrie**, his wife, 16 Mar 1739.

BOOTH, ALEXANDER, son of the late **Alexander B**, merchant in Aberdeen, 10 May 1742.

BOOTH, GEORGE, in Foggierigg, 16 Apr 1742.

BOWS, DUNCAN, in Hillock of Bucharn, 11 Jun 1748.

BOYN, MARJORY, late servant to Mr William Hay, minister at Cruden, 2 Jun 1747.

BRACO, JOHN, in Miln of Pettie, 15 Feb 1743.

BRADLEY, JOHN, sometime in Fordyce, 12 Oct 1750.

BRADSHAW, PETER, Lt in Col Hamilton's Regiment, 31 Jan 1735.

BRAND, ANN, see **Walter Brand**.

BRAND, WALTER, merchant, and late baillie of Cullen, and **Ann Brand** his daughter, 24 Jun 1747 and 16 Apr 1752.

BREBER, JOHN, in Balnacraig, 7 Jul 1747.

BREBNER, ELSPETH, in Blairdaff, widow of **Alexander Donald**, sometime tenant in Deuchries, 15 May 1750.

BREBNER, JAMES, in Towie of Clatt, 12 May 1750.

BREBNER, JEAN, see **Andrew Dyce**.

BRECK, JEAN, see **William Burnet**.

BREWSTER, JEAN, in Kirktoun of Fyvie, 25 Nov 1745.

BROADFOOT, PATRICK, Mr, student of Divinity in King's College, Aberdeen, 7 Jan 1742.

BRODIE, ALEXANDER, Lt, of HM ship *The Norfolk*, thereafter residing in Old Aberdeen, 12 Mar and 26 Nov 1750.

BRODIE, JOHN, carpenter in Aberdeen, 20 Feb 1754.

BROWN, ALEXANDER, of Nether Asleid, see **Jean Moir**.

BROWN, GEORGE, wright in Meadowhead of Mill of Fechill, 11 Sep 1740.

BROWN, GEORGE, in Smallburn of Auchterless, 19 May 1741.

BROWN, GEORGE, in Bridgehaugh, 7 Apr 1748.

BROWN, ISOBELL, in Wombelhill, 9 Jan 1751.

BROWN, JAMES, dyer in Aberdeen, 10 Aug 1747.

BROWN, JOHN, sometime in Easter Crichie, thereafter in Glack, 4 Dec 1753.

BROWN, JOHN, sometime quarrier at Glenquinthill, 30 Dec 1757.

BROWN, ROBERT, shipmaster in Aberdeen, 13 Apr 1736.

BROWNIE, JOHN, in Broomhill of Echt, 17 Jun 1740.

BROWNIE, MARGARET, widow of **John Mowat**, sometime at Mill of Glentown, in the parish of Monymusk, 31 Mar 1738.

BRUCE, JOHN, late in Lochhills, thereafter in Old Aberdeen, 27 Jan 1759.

BRYDIE, ALEXANDER and JOHN, both shipmasters in Peterhead, 8 May 1753.

BRYDIE, JOHN, see **Alexander Brydie**.

BUCHAN, GILBERT, mariner in Aberdeen, 24 Jun 1758.

BUCHAN, JAMES, sometime Lieutenant on board HM ship the "....", lately residing in Aberdeen, 21 Feb 1751.

BUCHAN, THOMAS, Maj Gen, at Ardlogie, 2 Sep 1728 and 25 Jun 1741.

BURNET, ALEXANDER, see **Robert Burnett**.

BURNET, ISOBELL, daughter of late **John B** sometime in Cannyglirach, 24 Jan 1754.

BURNET, ISOBELL, lawful daughter to late Mr **Robert B**, minister at Newhills, 17 May 1737.

BURNET, JAMES, Mr, of Mosston, minister at Ellon, 23 Jan 1745. See also **Margaret Burnet**.

BURNET, JAMES, and JEAN, lawful children to the late **Thomas B**, dyer in Abrdeen, 8 Mar 1735.

BURNET, JEAN, see **James Burnett**.

BURNET, JOHN, Mr, minister at Cluny, 26 Jun 1742.

BURNET, KATHARINE, Dame, widow of Sir **William Seton**, of Pitmedden, 31 Oct 1749.

BURNET, MARGARET, sister-german to late Mr **James B** minister at Ellon, 30 May 1746.

BURNET, ROBERT, see **Isobell Burnett**.

BURNET, ROBERT, son of **Alexander B**, in Upper Brathens, 17 Jun 1736.

BURNET, ROBERT, Mr, minister at Newhills, see **Elizabeth Thomson** and **Thomas B**.

BURNET, THOMAS, Sir, see Dame **Margaret Arbuthnot**.

BURNET, THOMAS, see **James Burnett**.

BURNET, THOMAS, lawful son to the late Mr **Robert B**, minister of Newhills, 2 Jun 1737.

BURNET, WILLIAM, cooper in Aberdeen, and **Jean Breck**, his wife, 28 Feb 1753.

BURTON, REBECCA, widow of Dr **George Gordon**, in Banff, 13 Jul 1737.

BUTE, ANNE, Countess of, wife of **Alexander Fraser** of Streichin, 12 Oct 1738.

BYRES, ANNE, residing at Glassiehillock in Newkirk, 5 Mar 1747.

BYRES, JEAN, widow of **William Souper**, merchant in Aberdeen, 31 May 1756.

BYRES, THOMAS, in Mill of Fuffle, 30 Jan 1735.

CAIRNY, JOHN, in Millbowie of Skene, 21 Aug 1753.

CAMPBELL, KATHARINE, Lady Craig, 30 Sept 1756.

CANTLY, ISOBELL, sometime wife to late **William Lawson**, weaver in Aberdeen, 10 Nov 1751.

CARNEGIE, ELSPETH, sometime servant, thereafter resident in Aberdeen, 29 Nov 1742.

CARNEGIE, JANET, Mrs, daughter of late Mr **Mungo C** sometime advocate in Edinburgh, 28 Jun 1754.

CARNEGIE, JEAN, widow of **John Forbes**, merchant in Aberdeen, 14 Jul 1740 and 27 Jul 1743.

CARNEGIE, JOHN, in Holemiln of Culture, 12 Mar 1750.

CARNEGIE, JOHN, dyer in Aberdeen, 28 Aug 1735.
CARNEGIE, MUNGO, see **Janet Carnegie.**
CASSIE, ANDREW, writer in Aberdeen, 24 Jun 1747.
CASSIE, ANDREW, sometime town-clerk of Old Aberdeen, see **Jean Stewart.**
CASSIE, ELIZABETH, in Mudhouse, 30 Mar 1737.
CATANACH, JOHN, alias **CATTO**, merchant in Ellon, 15 Jul 1742, 22 Dec 1749, and 28 Nov 1753.
CATANACH, ROBERT, merchant in Aberdeen, 19 Jan and 1 Mar 1738.
CAY, JOHN, in Hatton, 6 Mar 1751.
CAY, WILLIAM, tenant in Cocklaw, 16 Nov 1749.
CHALMERS, ALEXANDER, of Balnacraig, 6 Apr 1751.
CHALMERS, GEORGE, Mr, minister at Drumblade, see Mrs **Isobell Forbes.**
CHALMERS, GEORGE, Mr, principal of King's College of Aberdeen, 22 Oct 1746.
CHALMERS, JEAN, widow of **Arthur Dingwall**, sometime of Brownhill, 8 Feb 1750.
CHALMERS, JOHN, town-clerk of Ellon, 30 Apr 1740 and 15 Dec 1741.
CHALMERS, JOHN, wright in Aberdeen, 17 Mar 1748.
CHALMERS, ROBERT, Mr, sometime schoolmaster at Turriff, see **Isobell Peirie.**
CHARLES, ALEXANDER, advocate in Aberdeen, 20 Oct 1755.
CHARLES, JEAN, in Nether Kinknockie, 11 Aug 1741.
CHESSOR, GEORGE and JOHN, in Strathrey, lateley in Bogheads, 16 Dec 1740.
CHESSOR, GEORGE, in Strathrey, 23 Jul 1735.
CHESSOR, JOHN, see **George Chessor**.
CHEYN, MARGARET, in Slide, widow of **William Irvine**, sometime in Mill of Lethis, 24 Jul 1750.
CHEYNE, ROBERT, Mr, in Netherhill of St Fergus, 2 Aug 1745.
CHIVAS, JAMES, sometime shipmaster in Fraserburgh, 17 Feb 1759.
CHRISTALL, ANDREW, sometime in Graysford.   See **Christian Corrie**.
CHRISTALL, WILLIAM, wright in Aberdeen, 29 Nov 1748.
CHRISTIE, ALEXANDER, miller at Kildrummy, 3 Oct 1753.
CHRISTIE, DAVID, merchant in Aberdeen, 28 Jul 1743.
CHRISTIE, JOHN, in Kirkstyle of Gartly, see **George Ellis.**
CLARIHEW, ALEXANDER, in Old Keigg. See **Christian Ingram**.
CLARIHEW, CHARLES, in Scotsmill, 28 Nov 1758.
CLARK, ALEXANDER, shipmaster in Portsoy, 8 Apr 1742.
CLARK, GEORGE, sometime in Corsiestoun, see **Helen Imlay**.

CLARK, ISOBELL, sometime resident in Banff, thereafter in Bredach, 9 Mar 1758.

CLARK, JAMES, merchant in Old Aberdeen, 14 Aug 1742.

CLARK, JOHN, in Garden, and ISOBELL THOMSON, his wife, 1 Apr 1748.

CLARK, JOHN, merchant in Aberdeen, 12 Oct 1736.

CLARK, KATHARINE, in Oldtown of Aberdeen, daughter of late Mr Andrew C, minister at Methlick, 28 Jan 1748.

COBBAM, JEROM, merchant in Aberdeen, 25 Jul 1749.

COCK, JAMES, town-clerk of Banff, 10 Jul 1735.

COCKBURN, ALEXANDER, late merchant in Banff, 15 Jan 1754.

COOK, THOMAS, shoemaker in Cullen, 26 Mar 1751.

COPLAND, JAMES, in Bandley, 1 Jun 1745.

COPLAND, JAMES, in Backhill of Kinnellar, 20 May 1757.

COPLAND, JAMES, see Patrick Copland.

COPLAND, PATRICK, at Park, 7 Apr 1748.

COPLAND, PATRICK, Mr, late minister at Tough, and James C late in Warrachston, 29 Jan 1751.

CORRIE, CHRISTIAN, widow of Andrew Christall, sometime in Graysfoord, 26 Jul 1753.

COUTS, DAVID, wright in Aberdeen. See Isobell McConochie.

COUTS, FRANCIS, in Wateream, 8 Dec 1751.

COUTS, JAMES, merchant in Aberdeen, 7 Dec 1728, 11 Nov 1746 and 21 Apr 1747.

COUTS, JEAN, widow of William Thomson, merchant in Aberdeen, 7 May 1735.

COUTS, JOHN, in Greenflood of Fiddesbogg, 15 Apr 1742.

COUTS, PATRICK, in Old Grodie, 19 Oct 1758.

COW, GEORGE, post in Banff, 22 Jul 1740.

CRAIK, ALEXANDER, mariner in Fraserburgh, 15 Jun 1742.

CRAIK, ROBERT, mariner in Aberdeen, see Elspeth Littlejohn.

CRAWFORD, JAMES, shipmaster in Aberdeen, 6 Jan 1741, see also Mrs Elizabeth Keith.

CRICHTON, JANET, servant to Lady Bandon, elder, in Monealie, 31 Jan 1751.

CRICHTON, MAGDALEN, in Roundhill, widow of Alexander Stewart, sometime of Lesmurdie, 26 Oct 1736.

CROMAR, ANNA, widow of Alexander Middleton, sometime in Newtoun of Auchlossen, 9 Jan 1739.

CROMBIE, ALEXANDER, merchant in Aberdeen, 14 Nov 1751.

CROMBIE, RACHEL, see William Cushnie, also 14 Aug 1753.

CRUDEN, ANNE, daughter of late **Thomas C** in Craigellie and wife of **John Smith**, sometime in Cairnglass, now in Craigellie, 21 Jan 1755.

CRUDEN, DAVID, shipmaster in Aberdeen, 21 Jan 1755.

CRUDEN, JOHN, merchant in Aberdeen, lately residing at Newtoun of Streichin, 19 May 1740.

CRUDEN, THOMAS, late of Whitehill, parish of Streichin, 11 Feb 1744.

CRUDEN, THOMAS, in Craigelly, 6 Dec 1752, see also **Anne Cruden**.

CRUICKSHANK, ALEXANDER, in Mains of Iden, 22 Feb 1748.

CRUICKSHANK, ANNE, see **John Cruickshank**.

CRUICKSHANK, GEORGE, merchant, and late bailie in Aberdeen, 8 Apr 1737.

CRUICKSHANK, JAMES, merchant in Banff, 26 Sep 1743.

CRUICKSHANK, JAMES, of Monelie, see **Mary Cruickshank**.

CRUICKSHANK, JEAN, daughter of late **Alexander C** merchant in Inch, 10 Dec 1750.

CRUICKSHANK, JOHN, merchant in Banff, 5 Apr 1750.

CRUICKSHANK, JOHN, maltster and burgess of Aberdeen, **Mary Smith**, his widow, and **Anne C**, their daughter

CRUICKSHANK, MARY, widow of **William Smith**, late Baillie in Aberdeen, 18 Jun 1754.

CRUICKSHANK, MARY, only daughter of **James C**, of Monelie, 30 Sep 1736.

CRUICKSHANK, ROBERT, wright, burgess of Aberdeen, 23 Apr 1735.

CRUICKSHANK, WILLIAM, in Fingask, 7 Dec 1749.

CRUICKSHANK, WILLIAM, in Bogfowtown (fragment), 9 Jan 1735.

CRUICKSHANK, WILLIAM, in Oldtown of Atherb (Aucherb), 18 Jan 1739.

CULLEN, THOMAS, in Auchnamoon, 3 Oct 1740.

CUMING, ..., in Cullen. See **Margaret Gordon**.

CUMING, HELEN, in Clerkhill, 8 Feb 1759.

CUMING, JAMES, farmer in Sleepyhillock, 22 Nov 1744.

CUMING, JAMES, merchant in Aberdeen, 18 Jul 1749, see also **Helen Marr.**

CUMING, JAMES, alias **Gordon** of Birnes, 19 Dec 1752.

CUMING, JOHN GORDON, of Pitlurg, 20 Oct 1757.

CUMING, WILLIAM, sometime in Mosside of Pittuly, 6 Dec 1752.

CUSHNIE, JOHN, in Easter Cairny, 13 Jun 1749.

CUSHNIE, JOHN, in Quartans, 13 Sep 1755.

CUSHNIE, PATRICK, merchant in Aberdeen, 10 Aug 1745 and 14 Jan 1752.

CUSHNIE, WILLIAM, merchant in Aberdeen, and **Rachel Crombie**, his wife, 17 Jan 1752.

CUTHBERT, JOHN, in Newmiln of Boyne, 26 Jan 1744.

DALGARNO, JAMES, Mr, merchant in Old Aberdeen, 13 Dec 1743.

DARLING, JAMES, Mr, minister at Kintore, 4 May 1743.

DARRICK, BENJAMIN, Sergeant in Col Mark Kerr's Regiment of Foot, see **Helen Gordon**.

DAVIDSON, ALEXANDER, shipmaster in Aberdeen, 23 Feb 1740.

DAVIDSON, ALEXANDER, merchant in Old Meldrum, 26 Aug 1728 and 7 Oct 1740. See also **Jean Simpson**.

DAVIDSON, ELSPETH, daughter of late **George D**, farmer in Aberdeen, 21 Jun 1742.

DAVIDSON, GEORGE, see **Agnes Gray**.

DAVIDSON, GEORGE, see **Elspeth D**.

DAVIDSON, GEORGE, in Garriochsburn, 9 Feb 1759.

DAVIDSON, ISOBELL, widow of **George Stevenson**, late tenant in Sandend, 5 Dec 1749.

DAVIDSON, JAMES, shoemaker in Inverurie, 1 Jul 1736.

DAVIDSON, JOHN, sometime sailor in Aberdeen, 10 Dec 1739.

DAVIDSON, MARJORY, Lady, Cairnbrogie, and wife of late Mr **William Thain**, of Blackhall, her last husband, 17 Jun 1740.

DAVIDSON, MARJORY, widow of **James Alexander**, mason in Aberdeen, 2 Sep 1751.

DAVIE, JEAN, widow of **William Sym**, sometime merchant and bailie of Banff, 5 Jul 1750.

DAWSON, JOHN, in Mains of Iden, 15 Aug 1748.

DEMPSTER, MARGARET, widow of **James Meanie** in Melonside, 7 Jan 1743.

DEUCHAR, ALEXANDER, in Cullarly, 6 Sep 1744.

DEUCHAR, JOHN, in Garlogie, 16 Dec 1736.

DEY, ELIZABETH, late servant to Lord Braco, at Baldennie, 3 May 1755.

DICKIE, THOMAS, in Newseat, parish of Methlick, 12 Mar 1751.

DINGWALL, ANNE, daughter of late **Arthur D** sometime of Brownhill, 18 Dec 1746.

DINGWALL, ARTHUR, third son of **Arthur D**, of Brownhill, 24 Jul 1735 and 18 Dec 1738.

DINGWALL, LUCRETIA, wife of **William D** in Bracklay, 8 Jan 1747.

DINGWALL, WILLIAM, see **Lucretia Dingwall**.

DONALD, ALEXANDER, sometime tenant in Deuchries. See **Elspeth Brebner.**

DONALD, ANDREW, see **George Donald**.

DONALD, GEORGE, son of **Andrew D** in Brodiach, 7 Dec 1751.

DONALDSON, ANN, wife of **George Gordon**, late of Shillagreen, now in Little Cocklaw, 19 Jun 1747.

DONALDSON, JAMES, of Cocklaw, 18 Apr 1746.

DONALDSON, ROBERT, sailor in Aberdeen, 10 Feb 1749.

DONALDSON, ROBERT, merchant in Inverury, thereafter in Loanend of Kemnay, 12 Feb 1735.

DONALDSON, WILLIAM, shipmaster in Aberdeen, 28 Mar 1737.

DOUGLAS, JEAN, widow of **Robert Gellie**, merchant in Aberdeen, 19 Aug 1742.

DOUGLAS, MARY, daughter of **Robert D** of Bridgefoord, 23 Jun 1741.

DOUGLAS, ROBERT, see **Mary Douglas**.

DOWNIE, ALEXANDER, sometime tacksman of Kemnay, thereafter in Ardtaunies, and lastly in Whitehouse of Kemnay, 29 Dec 1747.

DOWNIE, BARBARA, daughter of late **Alexander D** weaver in Aberdour, 13 Jan 1748.

DOWNIE, JAMES, sometime merchant in Fraserburgh, 14 Nov 1743 and 18 Aug 1746.

DRUM, WILLIAM, in Lonhead of Pitmillen, 20 Feb 1748.

DUFF, JAMES, of Craigstone, 6 May 1736.

DUFF, MARGARET, youngest daughter of the late **William D**, of Whitehill, late provost of Banff, 13 Mar 1742.

DUFF, PATRICK, see **Thomas Duff**.

DUFF, ROBERT, sometime merchant in Banff, son of late **Thomas D**, sometime merchant there, 7 Apr 1748.

DUFF, THOMAS, eldest son of the second marriage of the late **Patrick D** of Craigstoun, 3 Oct 1737.

DUFF, WILLIAM, see **Margaret Duff**.

DUFFUS, ISOBELL, widow of **William Proctor**, late in Rothes, 6 Dec 1751.

DUFFUS, ROBERT, in Mains of Muchells, 17 Jun 1746.

DUFFUS, WILLIAM, in Bridgend, 27 Nov 1740.

DUGUID, JAMES, late in Slioch, and lastly in Inverkeithing, 15 Jun 1749.

DUGUID, MARY, see **John Grierson**.

DUGUID, ROBERT, of Auchenhove, 13 Dec 1739.

DUN, ALEXANDER, of Tarty, 18 Mar 1748.

DUN, GEORGE, sometime in Kamehill, see **Isobel Fraser**.

DUN, WILLIAM, in Uppertoun of Assloun, 13 Oct 1757.

DUNBAR, ARCHIBALD, see **James Dunbar**.

DUNBAR, ELIZABETH, in Buchraigie, widow of **Patrick Ogilvie**, sometime of Raggle, 7 Jun 1738.

DUNBAR, JAMES, Sir, of Durn, Baronet, 23 Dec 1737 and 14 Jan 1757.

DUNBAR, JAMES, second son of late **Archibald D** of Tillynaught, 13 Mar 1759.

DUNBAR, MARY, in Fordyce, widow of **James Ogilvie**, late of Toux, 17 Mar 1756.

DUNBAR, ROBERT, in Smidieboyn, 28 Nov 1738. See also **Mary Hay**.

DUNBAR, WILLIAM, Mr, of Grange, 17 Oct 1749, see also Mrs **May Arbuthnot**.

DUNCAN, ALEXANDER, late shipmaster in Portsoy, 24 May 1756.

DUNCAN, ALEXANDER, senior, merchant in Aberdeen, 28 Dec 1757.

DUNCAN, ALEXANDER, barber and periwig maker in Aberdeen, 25 Oct 1742.

DUNCAN, GEORGE, sometime merchant in Aberdeen, 27 Feb 1755. See also **Margaret Rolland**.

DUNCAN, ISOBELL, see **John Still**.

DUNCAN, JAMES, see **William Duncan**.

DUNCAN, JAMES, surgeon in Old Aberdeen, 8 Jan 1747.

DUNCAN, JOHN, in Daviot, see **Isobell Mark**.

DUNCAN, JOHN, Mr, late schoolmaster at Newhills, 2 Feb 1749.

DUNCAN, JOHN, in Mains of Montcoffer, 11 Nov 1751.

DUNCAN, JOHN, late tenant in Wester Beltie, thereafter in Millseat, parish of Kingedward, 19 Mar 1759.

DUNCAN, ROBERT, in Swelend, parish of Maryculter, 23 Dec 1746.

DUNCAN, WILLIAM, in Wester Collairly, 27 Feb 1753. See also **Isobell Fraser**.

DUNCAN, WILLIAM, late mariner on board the ship the *Leathly* of Aberdeen, and son of **James D** in Mains of Auchterellon, 15 Mar 1753.

DURNO, JOHN, in Mill of Barns, see **Isobell Anderson**.

DYCE, ALEXANDER, see **James Dyce**.

DYCE, ANDREW, Capt, shipmaster in Aberdeen, see also **Jean Brebner**, 28 Jan 1747.

DYCE, ANDREW, see **Katharine Dyce**.

DYCE, JAMES, lawful son of **Alexander D**, merchant in Aberdeen, 26 Nov 1737.

DYCE, JAMES, of Disblair, merchant in Aberdeen, 13 Feb 1751.

DYCE, KATHARINE and ANDREW, children of Mr **William D**, minister at Belhelvie, 27 Jun 1745.

EDWARD, GEORGE, in Quartans, 7 Oct 1743.

ELDER, JAMES, merchant in Banff, 18 Jul 1754.

ELLIS, ELIZABETH, see **George Ellis**.

ELLIS, GEORGE, at Milne of Knockleith, and **Elizabeth E** his eldest daughter, sometime wife of **John Christie**, in Kirkstyle of Gartly, 20 May 1741 and 8 Nov 1746.

ELLIS, THOMAS, sometime in Coattown of Nether-third, thereafter at Mill of Knockleith, parish of Auchterless, 22 Dec 1748.

ELLIS, WILLIAM, at Mill of Knockleith, 7 Dec 1756.

ELMSLIE, ELSPETH, widow of John Allan, sometime in Dorsinsilly, 27 Nov 1752.

ELMSLIE, ISOBELL, resident in Aberdeen, 23 Jun 1742.

FARQUHAR, ALEXANDER, sometime in Mains of Auchinhive, 9 Jul 1753.

FARQUHAR, FRANCIS, shipmaster in Aberdeen, 22 Jun 1758.

FARQUHAR, FRANCIS, Col, of Muniefarquhar, 16 Aug 1736.

FARQUHAR, JAMES, merchant in Portsoy, 15 Oct 1742 and 22 Jul 1748.

FARQUHAR, JOHN, in Mill of Auchinhove, 29 May 1746.

FARQUHAR, JOHN, elder and younger, in Mains of Wester Coul, 11 May 1750.

FARQUHAR, JOHN, Mr, sometime schoolmaster at Culross.   See **Barbara Garden**.

FARQUHAR, MARJORY, late in Cluny, 1 Oct 1742.

FARQUHAR, PATRICK, late in Priestwell, parish of Mortlick, 29 Apr 1752.

FARQUHAR, ROBERT, Mr, sometime bookseller in Aberdeen, 21 May 1753.

FARQUHARSON, ALEXANDER, in Tornygrach of Monaltry, 16 Mar 1749.

FARQUHARSON, CHARLES, of Inverey, WS, 16 Mar 1748, 6 Apr and 6 Aug 1751, 1 Aug 1752, 28 Jun and 20 Dec 1754, and 29 Apr 1755.

FARQUHARSON, DONALD, sometime in Bandley, thereafter in Hatton of Skene, and thereafter in Lairshill, 7 Sep 1753.

FARQUHARSON, DONALD, merchant in Tarland, sometime merchant in Aberdeen, 5 Dec 1758.

FARQUHARSON, EUPHAN, widow of **William Stewart** of Aucholly, 1 Feb 1750.

FARQUHARSON, JOHN, at Newkirk, 26 Mar 1757.

FARQUHARSON, JOHN, of Invercauld, 7 Aug 1758.

FARQUHARSON, PETER, see **Helen Forbes**.

FARQUHARSON, ROBERT, of Finzean, 22 Apr 1742.

FARQUHARSON, ROBERT, Mr, sometime minister at Kinnethmont. See **Margaret Leith**.

FARQUHARSON, WILLIAM, in Milnhead of Melgum, **Margaret Stewart**, his wife, afterwards wife of **Alexander Grant**, in Fechlie, and **Charles F**, their son, 4 Oct 1749, and 4 Apr 1766.   See also **Margaret Stewart**.

FERGUSON, ADAM, sometime in Inverury, 3 Jun 1757.

FERGUSON, ALEXANDER, shipmaster in Peterhead, 26 Jan 1744.

FERGUSON, GEORGE, sometime in Kilnary, 31 Mar 1741.

FERGUSON, HENRY, sometime dyer in Tarland, thereafter in Auchindore, 28 Jan 1747.

FERGUSON, JAMES, cooper in Aberdeen, 6 Jul 1737.

FERGUSON, JOHN, in Glenmilne of Johnsleys, 28 Mar 1759.

FERGUSON, MARY, former resident of Old Meldrum, 19 Jun 1755.

FERGUSON, WILLIAM, at Mill of Inch, 22 Nov 1748.

FERGUSON, WILLIAM, shoemaker, burgess in Inverurie, 17 Jul 1738.

FETTES, JANET, in Cottardern, 12 Mar 1736.

FIDDES, JAMES, merchant in Newburgh of Foveran, 29 May 1746.

FINDLATER, JAMES, sometime merchant in London, 21 Jul 1739.

FINDLAY, ELIZABETH, resident in Fraserburgh, 27 Jan 1747.

FINDLAY, ISABELL, see **Thomas Ironside**.

FINDLAY, JAMES, tenant in Baads, 26 Jun 1754.

FINNIE, ALEXANDER, late resident in Aberdeen. See **Katharine Dyce**.

FINNIE, JAMES, merchant in Aberdeen, 23 Mar 1736.

FINNIE, MARGARET, widow of **James Gray**, elder, shoemaker in Banff, 2 Jul 1722 and 30 Jan 1753.

FINNIE, THOMAS, of Bonakettle, merchant in Aberdeen, 1740 and 12 Jun 1749.

FINNIE, THOMAS, merchant in Aberdeen. See **Margaret Skene**.

FINNIE, WILLIAM, merchant in Aberdeen, 20 Nov 1739.

FLETCHER, PATRICK, sometime in Newtoun of Glentanner, 18 Jan 1737.

FOORD, MARGARET, in Drumniachie, 28 Jul 1749.

FORBES, ALEXANDER, tidewaiter at Portknockie, 14 Feb 1740.

FORBES, ALEXANDER, of Ludquharn, 22 Dec 1741.

FORBES, ALEXANDER, Locharmick, merchant in Aberdeen, 31 May 1738 and 9 Mar 1749. See also **Janet Gordon**.

FORBES, ALEXANDER, of Blackford, 20 Jun 1751, 17 Jul 1753, and 10 May 1760. See also **Helen Gellie.**

FORBES, ALEXANDER, in Torndahuish, thereafter in Burnside, 2 Oct 1755.

FORBES, ALEXANDER, Mr, minister at Forgue, 13 Apr 1759.

FORBES, ARTHUR, Mr, sometime minister at Oyn, 7 Feb 1730, 3 Dec 1734, and 2 Jun 1742.

FORBES, ARTHUR, Mr, of Shivas, 12 May 1744.

FORBES, ARTHUR, in Lairshill, sometime in Bandley, 28 Jan 1755.

FORBES, ARTHUR, Sir, see Dame **Christian Ross**.

FORBES, ARTHUR, late factor of Cursinday, 23 Aug 1737.

FORBES, BARBARA, daughter of late **John F** of Auquhorties, 6 May 1746.

FORBES, BARBARA, daughter of late **Alexander F** of Blackford, 21 Jun 1757.

FORBES, BARBARA, daughter to the late **John F** of Leslie, 15 Mar 1739.

FORBES, ELIZABETH, Mrs, daughter of late **Alexander F** of Balogie, 9 Apr 1752.

FORBES, GEORGE, of Alford, 19 Jan 1742.

FORBES, HELEN, sometime wife to **Peter Farquharson**, in Millton of Auchoillie, and third daughter of late **John F** of Lodmacay, 18 Jul 1749.

FORBES, ISABELL, Mrs, widow of Mr **George Chalmers**, minister at Drumblade, 2 Jun 1743.

FORBES, JANET, see **William Bonnar.**

FORBES, JEAN, Lady, Badyfurrow, 18 Aug 1740.

FORBES, JOHN, merchant in Aberdeen, see **Jean Carnegie.**

FORBES, JOHN, Capt, of Boyndlie, 12 Feb 1741.

FORBES, JOHN, eldest lawful son of **William F** of Tornaboon, 21 Jun 1750.

FORBES, JOHN, mariner in Aberdeen, son of **John F** in Kincardine, 24 Dec 1750.

FORBES, JOHN, of Belnaboddach, 6 Feb 1752.

FORBES, JOHN, advocate in Aberdeen, 6 Feb 1752.

FORBES, JOHN, of Leslie, see **Barbara Forbes.**

FORBES, JOHN, of Deskrie, 22 Dec 1737.

FORBES, LAUCHLAN, of Edinglassie, 12 Mar 1753.

FORBES, MARGARET, lawful daughter of **Harry F** of Boyndlie, 12 Aug 1741.

FORBES, MARJORY, see **Thomas Lumsden.**

FORBES, PATRICK, of Schivas, 12 May 1744.

FORBES, ROBERT, in Whitewall, 25 Jun 1741.

FORBES, SAMUEL, Sir, of Foveran, 10 Jan 1727 and 4 Aug 1743.

FORBES, SAMUEL, of Knaperny, 10 Feb 1749.

FORBES, THOMAS, of Waterton, 2 Apr 1731 and 10 Mar 1735.

FORBES, WILLIAM, Mr, minister of Tarves, 31 May 1739.

FORBES, WILLIAM, Lord, 20 Jan 1732 and 19 Jun 1742.

FORBES, WILLIAM, of Badyfurrow, 18 Aug 1740.

FORBES, WILLIAM, of Disblair, 9 Jan 1741.

FORBES, WILLIAM, Sir, advocate, Professor of Civil Law in King's College, Aberdeen, 25 Jul 1743.

FORBES, WILLIAM, of Tilliory, 27 Jun 1746.

FORBES, WILLIAM, in Bellachallich of Crathie, 11 Jun 1751.

FORBES, WILLIAM, see Dame **Margaret Rose.**

FORD, MARGARET, only lawful daughter of **William F** in Milnfoot of Glentanner, and now resident in Aberdeen, 10 Jan 1744.

FORD, WILLIAM, in Belnacraig, 4 Feb 1742.

FORDYCE, ALEXANDER, in Broadmuir of Cruden, 18 Mar (1738) 1737.

FORDYCE, DAVID, Mr, lately Professor of Philosophy in Marishall College, Aberdeen, 10 Mar 1752, 4 Oct 1755 and 1 Jul 1756.

FORDYCE, GEORGE, merchant in Aberdeen, eldest son of the late **George F** sometime provost of Aberdeen, 10 Nov 1736 and 11 Dec 1746.

FORDYCE, JOHN, of Gask, merchant in Turriff, 19 Jan 1737.

FORDYCE, KATHARINE, daughter of late **George F**, sometime provost of Aberdeen, 16 Apr 1742.

FORREST, ANNE, in Burnhead, 29 Jun 1756.

FORREST, WILLIAM, merchant, and late bailie of Fraserburgh, 30 Nov 1738.

FORSYTH, ALEXANDER, in Culbuichly, 16 Aug 1745.

FORSYTH, WILLIAM, sometime in Callenard, thereafter in Poddocklaw, 21 Jan 1741.

FOTHERINGHAM, CHARLES, Dr, physician in Banff, 14 May 1747.

FOWLIE, JAMES, in Bartholl Chapell, 18 Jun 1741.

FRASER, ALEXANDER, Mr, of Powis, sub-principal of King's College of Aberdeen, and Mr **Alexander F** younger, of P, late civilist in said College, 6 Apr 1742.

FRASER, ALEXANDER, sometime officer of Excise at Aberdeen, 6 Feb 1744.

FRASER, ALEXANDER, of Streichin, see **Anne Bute**.

FRASER, BATHIA, daughter of late Mr **George F**, sub-principal in King's College, Aberdeen, 18 Sep 1744.

FRASER, FRANCIS, in Burnside of Lumphanan, 24 Nov 1757.

FRASER, GEORGE, see **Bathia Fraser**.

FRASER, HUGH, of Kinnaires, see Lady **Margaret Leslie**.

FRASER, ISOBELL, wife of late **George Dun**, sometime in Kamehill, and **William Duncan**, in Wester Collarly, 19 Aug 1743.

FRASER, JAMES, sometime in North Essie, 21 Jan 1742.

FRASER, JAMES, son of **Simon F**, in Newton of Auchiries, 30 Sep 1742.

FRASER, JOHN, sometime in Kinguidy, parish of Bourty, 20 Jun 1745.

FRASER, JOHN, in Cottartoun of Ardoch, 14 Nov 1754.

FRASER, JOHN, sometime shipmaster in Fraserburgh, 17 Nov 1757

FRASER, JOHN, merchant in Old Aberdeen, 15 Apr 1736.

FRASER, SIMON, see **James Fraser**.

FRASER, WILLIAM, at Mill of Clola, 7 May 1741.

FRASER, WILLIAM, sometime at Stonemill of Inverugie, 19 Feb 1750.

FROSTER, GEORGE, in Balquhainachie, 2 May 1737.

FYFE, WILLIAM, dyer in Turriff, 2 Jan 1722 and 15 Jan 1737.

GALL, ALEXANDER, in town of Raithen, 15 Mar 1739.

GALL, JOHN, merchant in Aberdeen, 25 Aug 1736.

GARDEN, AGNES, widow of **Alexander Rae** in Kinaldie, 7 Apr 1747.

GARDEN, BARBARA, widow of Mr **John Farquhar**, sometime schoolmaster at Culross, 24 Nov 1755.

GARDEN, GEORGE, merchant, and sometime provost and bailie of Banff, 21 Feb 1740, 17 Jul and 19 Aug 1745.

GARDEN, GEORGE, schoolmaster in Aberdeen, 23 Feb 1738.

GARRIOCH, ALEXANDER, see **Marjory Garrioch**.

GARRIOCH, MARJORY, widow of Mr **Robert Strachan** of Tillieriach, and **Alexander S**, her son.

GARRIOCH, WILLIAM, merchant in Tarland, 1 Aug 1739.

GARRIOCH, WILLIAM, of Tilliehettie, 2 Jun 1748.

GARRIOCH, WILLIAM, merchant in Ellon, 6 Dec 1751.

GARVOCK, WILLIAM, Mr, in Dykeside of Towie, 28 Oct 1742.

GAVIN, JAMES, in Kirktoun of Echt, 15 Apr 1748.

GEE, JOHN, collector of Excise at Aberdeen, living at Hillton, 3 Aug 1749.

GELLIE, JAMES, sometime tide surveyor, now land surveyor at Aberdeen. See **Elizabeth Thomson**.

GELLIE, PATRICK, merchant and bailie in Aberdeen, 18 Jul 1743.

GELLIE, ROBERT, merchant in Aberdeen, 12 Nov 1737 and 23 Jul 1752, see also **Jean Douglas** and **Margaret Ross** (19 Aug 1742).

GELLIE, WILLIAM, Mr, merchant and late bailie of Aberdeen, 21 Feb 1740.

GEORGE, DAVID, merchant in Aberdeen, 4 Oct 1722, 26 Jan 1731 and 7 Sep 1742.

GERARD, GILBERT, Mr, minister at Chapel of Garioch, 13 Mar 1738.

GERARD, JAMES, in Turriff, 2 Oct 1755.

GERARD, WILLIAM, sometime in Blackhouse, son of the late **William G**, in Walkerhill, 27 Nov 1735.

GIBB, JAMES, in Murthill, 21 Mar 1739.

GIBB, MARGARET, resident in Aberdeen, 5 Jun 1748.

GIBSON, JOHN, in Nether Leask, see also **Agnes Barnet**, 19 Jul 1744.

GILL, GEORGE, shipmaster in Fraserburgh, 21 Jun 1742.

GILLENDERS, ALEXANDER, in Tilliechardich, 27 Oct 1737.

GILLENDERS, MALCOLM, in Tilliefoudy, parish of Aboyne, 29 Jan 1743.

GILLENDERS, MARGARET, sometime at Finzean, 12 Sep 1755.

GILLET, JOHN, weaver near Culture, 25 Sep 1749.

GLEN, JAMES, sometime in Blackton, parish of Alva, 2 Jun 1752.

GLENNY, ALEXANDER, in Denmilne of Cultur, 13 Aug 1742.

GLENNY, ANN, see **William Glenny**.

GLENNY, JOHN, late merchant in Aberdeen, son of **Thomas G**, merchant there, 23 Sep 1749.

GLENNY, JOHN, in Mains of Strathlock, see **Christian Barron**.

GLENNY, WILLIAM, sometime in Newark, and **William** and **Ann G**, his children, 20 Jul 1742.

GOODALL, PATRICK, late in Culphin, 7 Apr 1748.

GORDON, ALEXANDER, of Barrack, see **Isobell Udny**.

GORDON, ALEXANDER, of Kinmundy, 8 Feb 1737.

GORDON, ALEXANDER, bookbinder in Aberdeen, see **Isobell Largoe**.

GORDON, ALEXANDER, Mr, minister at Foveran, 3 Jul 1746.

GORDON, ALEXANDER, in Crofts of Glenbucket, 24 Aug 1750.

GORDON, ALEXANDER, in Aldihash, parish of Glenmuick, merchant in Aberdeen, 27 Feb 1752.

GORDON, ALEXANDER, see **Elizabeth Gordon**.

GORDON, ALEXANDER, of Pitlurg, see **Mrs Elizabeth Gordon**.

GORDON, BARBARA, Mrs, daughter of the late **Francis G** of Craig, 13 Dec 1737.

GORDON, CECILIA, Mrs, widow of **Robert G**, of Cairnfield, 10 Jan 1749.

GORDON, CHARLES, of Buthlaw, advocate in Aberdeen, 13 Nov 1752.

GORDON, CHRISTIAN, wife of Mr **Robert Leslie**, in Kinninoy, and the said **Mr Robert Leslie**, 26 Aug 1747.

GORDON, DAVID, in Kirkhill, 25 Nov 1746.

GORDON, ELIZABETH, Mrs, daughter of **Alexander G** of Pitlurg, 9 Aug 1744.

GORDON, ELIZABETH, lawful daughter to late **John G** of Auchluchries, and wife to **Alexander G** now of Auchluchries, 19 Jan 1739.

GORDON, FRANCIS, see **Mrs Barbara Gordon**.

GORDON, FRANCIS, of Mill of Kincardine, 3 Sep 1748.

GORDON, GEORGE, see **Rebecca Burton**.

GORDON, GEORGE, late of Shillagreen, now in Little Cocklaw, see **Ann Donaldson**.

GORDON, GEORGE, of Buckie, 13 May 1729, 4 Feb and 28 Apr 1732, 15 Oct 1734 and 21 Dec 1756.

GORDON, GEORGE, of Shilagreen, 9 Apr 1747.

GORDON, GEORGE, stampmaster in Aberdeen, 10 Mar 1755.

GORDON, HELEN, resident in Banff, 2 Jun 1748.

GORDON, HELEN, wife to **Benjamin Darrick**, sergeant in the Regiment of Foot commanded by Col Mark Kerr, 21 Mar 1738.

GORDON, HUGH, in Sachinloan, 26 Feb 1751.

GORDON, JAMES, of Ellon, sometime merchant in Edinburgh, and **James Gordon**, his son, 1 Sep 1732, 26 Jan 1734, 29 Sep 1740, and 26 Sep 1759.

GORDON, JAMES, of Beldornie, 13 Mar 1741.

GORDON, JAMES, of Meiklemill of Esslemont, 23 Dec 1743.

GORDON, JAMES, Dr, see **Margaret Baird**.

GORDON, JAMES, of Banchory, 18 Oct 1751 and 20 Jun 1753.

GORDON, JAMES, merchant in Banff, 22 Jan 1753.

GORDON, JAMES, sometime merchant in Portsoy, 8 Apr 1754.

GORDON, JAMES, of Cocklaw, 19 Sep 1755.

GORDON, JAMES, Dr, of Pitlurg, 15 Jan 1756.

GORDON, JAMES, merchant in Peterhead, 1 Jul 1756.

GORDON, JAMES, see **Lewis Gordon**.

GORDON, JAMES, Sir, of Park, 25 Aug 1730, 8 Nov 1733, 16 Apr 1734, 28 Apr and 6 May 1735.

GORDON, JAMES, of Balbithan, 18 Nov 1736.

GORDON, JANET, widow of **Alexander Forbes**, Lochermick, merchant in Aberdeen, 1 Nov 1750.

GORDON, JEAN, daughter of late **Patrick G**, of Hallhead, and widow of Mr **Alexander Sherriff**, writer in Edinburgh, 29 Jul 1742 and 10 Jun 1743.

GORDON, JOHN, see **Elizabeth Gordon**.

GORDON, JOHN, of Craig, 18 Dec 1740, 25 Oct 1749, 19 Feb and 31 Jul 1750.

GORDON, JOHN, of Wardhouse, 29 Dec 1740 and 22 Feb 1753.

GORDON, JOHN, in Muir of Tullich, 19 Feb 1742.

GORDON, JOHN, sometime in Bogstoun, 14 Aug 1751.

GORDON, JOHN, see **William Gordon**.

GORDON, JOHN, late tenant on Woodhead of Fetterletter, 14 Oct 1736.

GORDON, JOHN, Dr, of Hiltoun, physician in Aberdeen, 5 May 1737.

GORDON, LEWIS, of Kinmundy, son of late Mr **James G**, parson of Rothiemay, 25 Sep and 6 Nov 1736 and 28 Jan 1743.

GORDON, LEWIS, of Achmull, merchant in Aberdeen, 24 Jan 1744.

GORDON, LEWIS, wright in Aberdeen, 20 Mar 1735.

GORDON, MARGARET, Lady, daughter of the late **George**, Earl of Aberdeen, 2 Jun 1741.

GORDON, MARGARET, see **William Jameson**.

GORDON, MARGARET, see Mr **Alexander Tosh**.

GORDON, MARGARET, youngest of late **Alexander G**, of Logie, 17 Dec 1751.

GORDON, MARGARET, widow of .... Cuming, in Cullen, 9 Aug 1753.

GORDON, PATRICK, see **Jean Gordon**.

GORDON, PETER, of Abergeldie, 29 Nov 1735, 24 Mar 1737 and 11 Mar 1740.

GORDON, PETER, in Crofts of Glenbucket, 14 Jun 1750.

GORDON, ROBERT, see Mrs **Cecilia Gordon**.

GORDON, ROBERT, of Cairnfield, 10 Nov 1736.

GORDON, THOMAS, shipmaster at Aberdeen, 9 Jul 1752.

GORDON, THOMAS, junior, merchant in Aberdeen, 17 May 1756.

GORDON, WALTER, shipmaster in Aberdeen, 4 Jan 1757.

GORDON, WILLIAM, in Pieriesmill, 11 Jan 1735.

GORDON, WILLIAM, merchant in Banff, 27 Aug 1742 and 15 Feb 1748.

GORDON, WILLIAM, merchant in Aberdeen, 21 Nov 1748.

GORDON, WILLIAM, wright in Blackhall, 16 Nov 1752.

GORDON, WILLIAM, Sir, of Lesmore, Bart, 24 Nov 1752.

GORDON, WILLIAM, late of Govell, sometime quartermaster in Lord Shannon's Regiment of Foot, 7 Mar 1755.

GORDON, WILLIAM, son of late **John G**, of Wardhouse, 6 May 1756 and 29 Nov 1757.

GOW, MARGARET, widow of **Alexander Lind** in Tarves, 3 May 1742.

GRAHAM, JEAN, widow of **Joseph G**, late merchant in London, 9 Aug 1736.

GRAHAM, JOSEPH, see **Jean Graham**.

GRANT, ALEXANDER, in Glencarvie, afterwards in Fechlie.   See **Margaret Stewart**.

GRANT, FRANCIS, see **Anna Anderson**.

GRANT, HUGH, Capt, in Kinnord, 12 Oct 1752.

GRANT, ISOBELL, only lawful daughter of late **James G**, sometime in Carnaqual, 19 Dec 1750.

GRANT, JAMES, at Mill of Logie, 28 Jul 1740.

GRANT, JAMES, see **Isobell Grant**.

GRANT, JAMES, farmer in Woodhead, in parish of Fintray, 17 Nov 1753.

GRANT, JOHN, Lt, sometime in Fishrie, thereafter in Pittendrum, 12 Jul 1739.

GRANT, PETER, at Bridgend of Fyvie, 19 Jun 1746.

GRANT, WILLIAM, sometime chapman in Ballachduie, in parish of Glenbucket, 22 Apr 1747.

GRANT, WILLIAM, in Mosside of Faichill, 27 Jun 1754.

GRAY, AGNES, wife of **George Davidson**, in Kintore, 3 Jun 1736.

GRAY, GEORGE, merchant in Boghouse, 17 Nov 1747.

GRAY, JAMES, elder, shoemaker in Banff. See **Margaret Finnie**.

GRAY, JAMES, sometime in Spittlehaugh of Glenmuick, 6 Apr 1751.

GRAY, JAMES, merchant in Aberdeen, 22 Nov 1737.

GRAY, JOHN, late in Mains of Glassa, 18 May 1748.

GRAY, JOHN, in Newtown of Pitblain, 11 Jul 1754.

GRAY, JOHN, in Mill of Minony, 9 Mar 1758.

GRAY, PATRICK, wright in Aberdeen, 13 Nov 1736.

GRAY, PETER, in Garronhead, 19 Nov 1746.

GRAY, WILLIAM, in Auphorsk, 10 May 1744.

GRAY, WILLIAM, sometime weaver in Inverury, 4 Jul 1748.

GREGORY, JAMES, Dr, Professor of Medicine in the King's College of Aberdeen, 15 Jun 1733, 24 Feb 1744 and 20 Jul 1756.

GREIG, ANDREW, sometime shipmaster in Fraserburgh, 6 Jun 1751.

GREIG, JAMES, farmer in Old Aberdeen, 14 Nov 1754.

GREIRSON, JOHN, in Loanhead of Auchinhove, and **Mary Duguid**, his widow, 9 Nov 1750.

GRUB, ROBERT, in Frosterhill, 19 Dec 1752.

GUIES, DAVID, see **David McDonald**.

GUTHRIE, GEORGE, merchant tailor in Cullen, 7 Sep 1759.

GUTHRIE, HELEN, eldest daughter of late **Thomas G**, of Blackhouse, 8 Feb 1757.

GUTHRIE, JOHN, Sir, of Kingedward, 17 Dec 1722, 16 Jun 1725 and 14 Jul 1737.

GUTHRIE, JOHN, in Pittendrum, 3 Apr 1728 and 5 Oct 1743.

GUTHRIE, THOMAS, see **Helen Guthrie**.

GUTHRIE, THOMAS, Mr, of Blackhouse, 8 May 1735.

HALKET, GEORGE, in Gelliemill, 17 Nov 1736.

HALL, GEORGE, in Newtoun of Premnay, 3 Jul 1740.

HAMILTON, DANIEL, of Shelochsley, merchant in Aberdeen, 1 Feb 1750.

HAMILTON, JOHN, sometime in Upper Clochan, 16 Nov 1738.

HAMLIN, SAMUEL, woolcomber in Aberdeen, 11 Apr 1745.

HARROW, ANDREW, mariner in Aberdeen, see **Helen Nicolson**.

HARROW, JAMES, gardener in Aberdeen. See **Elspeth Melvin**.

HARVIE, JANET, widow of **Anthony Imray**, sometime in Hirn, 12 Sep 1751.

HATT, WILLIAM, merchant in Old Aberdeen, 30 May 1735.

HAY, ANDREW, of Montblary, WS, 23 Apr and 17 Jun 1751.

HAY, ANNA, see Mr **Hugh Hay**.

HAY, CHARLES, of Rannes, 9 Mar 1752, 12 Aug 1756, and 2 Sep 1758.

HAY, COLIN, JOHN, JAMES, GILBERT and VIOLET, children of late Mr **Thomas H**, sheriff-clerk of Aberdeen, 22 Dec 1748.

HAY, GEORGE, Mr, late minister at Newdurn, 27 Feb 1739.

HAY, GILBERT, see **Colin Hay**.

HAY, GILBERT, in Auchirie of Cruden, 10 Feb 1756.

HAY, HUGH, wright in Old Aberdeen, 26 Apr 1759.

HAY, JAMES, see **Colin Hay**.

HAY, JEAN, widow of **John Lorimer**, writer in Cullen, 17 Dec 1754.
HAY, JOHN, of Aquharnie, 29 Jan 1756.
HAY, JOHN, see **Colin Hay**.
HAY, THOMAS, Mr, sometime sheriff-clerk of Aberdeen, 6 Dec 1745 and 13 Nov 1752.
HAY, VIOLET, see **Colin Hay**.
HAY, WILLIAM, late tutor of Ranes, 22 Jan 1734 and 1 Nov 1739.
HAY, WILLIAM, of Balbithen, see **Barbara Menzies**.
HECTOR, DAVID, workman in Aberdeen, 17 Oct 1749.
HENDERSON, ALEXANDER, in Milntoun of Atherb, 8 Dec 1739.
HENDERSON, WILLIAM, at Mill of Tillinamont, 6 Jul 1738.
HEPBURN, WILLIAM, merchant in Aberdeen, 24 Jan 1751.
HILL, JAMES, merchant in Old Aberdeen, 20 May 1746.
HILTON, ANNE, widow of **Andrew Wilson**, sometime at Rhannis, 19 May 1751.
HOUSTON, WILLIAM, Mr, feuar in Fraserburgh, 10 Jun 1754.
HOWIE, ALEXANDER, sometime in Little Cushnie, parish of Auchterless, 31 Mar 1759.
HOWIESON, ANDREW, Mr, one of the masters of the Grammar School of Aberdeen, 9 Feb and 7 Dec 1749.
HUIE, JOHN, in Dummuies, parish of Drumblade, see **Christian Mitchell**.
HUNTER, ALEXANDER, in Bervie, 31 Jan 1747.
HUNTER, WILLIAM, sometime in Candieglirach, 11 Oct 1743.
IMLAY, HELEN, widow of **George Clark**, sometime in Corsiestoun, 29 Jan 1743.
IMRIE, ANTHONY, sometime in Hirn. See **Janet Harvie**.
INGRAM, ALEXANDER, see **William Ingram**.
INGRAM, CHRISTIAN, first wife of **Alexander Clarihew**, in Old Keigg, 26 Feb 1751.
INGRAM, JOHN, gardener in Aberdeen, 26 Aug 1743.
INGRAM, MARGARET, first wife of **James Milne**, late in Newton of Knockespack, now in Mill of Montgarry, 26 Feb 1751.
INGRAM, WILLIAM, son of late **Alexander I**, in Blackhillocks, 12 Nov 1742.
INGRAM, WILLIAM, in Drumgowan, and **Elizabeth Anderson**, sometime his wife, thereafter wife to also late **Francis Spence**, in Christ's Kirk, and **Elspet Spence**, his daughter, 19 Jul 1745.
INNES, ALEXANDER, Mr, Professor of Philosophy in Marishall College of Aberdeen, 2 Nov 1742.
INNES, ELSPETH, see **George Riddoch**.
INNES, GEORGE, in Littlewrangam, 16 Dec 1742.

INNES, HUGH, Mr, sometime minister at Mortlack.   See **Elizabeth Abernethy**.

INNES, JAMES, Mr, late minister at Banff, 15 Apr 1754.

INNES, JEAN, wife to **John Paton**, in Mains of Elrick, 19 Apr 1748.

INNES, JOHN, Mr, sometime minister at Garnery, 25 Mar 1741.

INNES, JOHN, wright in Aberdeen, 8 Feb 1754.

INNES, MARGARET, see **Thomas Taylor**.

INNES, PATRICK, in Nether Ardwell, 22 Jul 1735.

INNES, ROBERT, Mr, minister at Udny, 15 Nov 1755.

INNES, THOMAS, mariner in Aberdeen, 3 Jun 1741.

INNES, WILLIAM, Mr, late minister at Skene, 13 Apr 1756.

IRONSIDE, THOMAS, in Fiddesbeg, and **Isabell Findlay**, his wife, 30 Jun 1741.

IRVINE, ALEXANDER, Mr, of Saphock, 31 Oct 1755.

IRVINE, ALEXANDER, in Pitmuckstone, 2 Dec 1755.

IRVINE, ALEXANDER RAMSAY, see **Mary Irvine**.

IRVINE, ALEXANDER, see Mrs **Margaret Irvine**.

IRVINE, ANNE, widow of **James Mercer**, merchant in Aberdeen, 28 Oct 1737.

IRVINE, HELEN, widow of **Alexander Walker**, late provost of Aberdeen, 15 Jul 1756.

IRVINE, JAMES, advocate in Aberdeen (wanting), 23 Jun 1738.

IRVINE, JEAN, wife of Mr **John Kennedy**, sometime minister at Peterculter, 18 Jun 1730 and 12 Feb 1741.

IRVINE, JOHN, of Drum, 1 Feb 1738.

IRVINE, KENNETH, shipmaster in Aberdeen, 31 Jul 1744.

IRVINE, MARGARET, Mrs, daughter of **Alexander I**, of Drum, 19 Dec 1747 and 15 Apr 1751.

IRVINE, MARY, only lawful daughter of late **Alexander I**, of Saphock, and wife of **Alexander Ramsay I**, now of Saphock, 20 Mar 1750.

IRVINE, WILLIAM, late tenant in Mill of Laithers, 21 Nov 1748.

IRVINE, WILLIAM, sometime in Mill of Lethis.   See **Margaret Cheyn**.

JACK, ALEXANDER, sometime in Middle Ardiffray, 4 Jun 1744.

JACKSON, GEORGE, sometime at Mill of Cairden, 27 Feb 1751.

JACKSON, JOHN, in Mill of Cairden, 27 Feb 1751.

JAFFRAY, ANDREW, see **Helen Jaffray**.

JAFFRAY, DAVID, lawful son of late **David J**, merchant in Aberdeen, 2 Jan 1735.

JAFFRAY, GEORGE, feuar and farmer in Fraserburgh, 7 Dec 1749.

JAFFRAY, HELEN, daughter to late **Andrew J**, merchant in Aberdeen, 12 Feb 1747 and 7 Jan 1748.

JAMIESON, ALEXANDER, son of late **William J**, sometime in Welltoun of Stonywood, 2 Jan 1744.

JAMIESON, ANNE, in Bogs of Skilly, widow of **Robert J**, sometime tenant there, 5 Aug 1756.

JAMIESON, JAMES, maltman in Old Aberdeen, 25 Jul 1751.

JAMIESON, JOHN, sometime in Birkhall, 27 Nov 1752.

JAMIESON, ROBERT, see **Anne Jamieson**.

JAMIESON, WILLIAM, in Walltoun of Stonywood, 22 Oct 1743.

JAMIESON, WILLIAM, see **Alexander Jamieson**.

JAMIESON, WILLIAM, in Fordyce, 13 Feb 1751.

JAMIESON, WILLIAM, in Mill of Fowlis, and **Margaret Gordon**, his wife, 10 Apr 1735.

JEANS, WILLIAM, merchant in Old Aberdeen, see **Jean Panton**.

JOHNSTON, GEORGE, sailor in Aberdeen, 30 Nov 1738.

JOHNSTON, ROBERT, at Midmiln of Cruden, 26 Jan 1747.

JOHNSTON, WILLIAM, maltster in Aberdeen, 12 Jun 1759.

JOLLY, WILLIAM, in Beanshill, 8 Dec 1755.

JOPP, ANDREW, merchant in Inch, 27 Apr 1742 and 18 May 1747.

JOSS, JOHN, of Colleonard, 8 Nov 1743.

KEIR, JAMES, portioner of Reinlone, 25 Jun 1741.

KEIR, JOHN, in Delnaboe, 26 Feb 1747.

KEITH, GEORGE, sometime merchant in Fraserburgh, 4 Jun 1748.

KEITH, GEORGE, advocate in Aberdeen, 30 Nov 1738 and 7 Sep 1742.

KEITH, GEORGE, of Whiteriggs and Knox, 4 Mar 1754.

KEITH, JAMES, of Crichie, see **Margaret Gordon**, 5 Dec 1728, 20 Sep 1733 and 15 Dec 1738.

KEITH, MARY, in Saplingbrae, 24 Jul 1735.

KEITH, WILLIAM, in Tilliekiro, 13 Aug 1742.

KENNEDY, ANNE, daughter of late Mr **John K**, sometime minister at Peterculter, 12 Feb 1741.

KENNEDY, JOHN, see **Anne Kennedy**, **Mary Kennedy**, **William Kennedy**, and **John Kennedy**.

KENNEDY, JOHN, lawful son of late Mr **John K**, sometime minister at Peterculter, 12 Feb 1741.

KENNEDY, JOHN, Mr, see **Jean Irvine**.

KENNEDY, MARY, Mrs, daughter of late Mr **John K**, sometime minister at Peterculter, and wife of **John Rollo**, second son of **Robert**, Lord Rollo, 29 Aug 1751.

KENNEDY, WILLIAM, son of late Mr **John K**, sometime minister at Peterculter, 12 Feb 1741.

KER (KERR), ALEXANDER, of Meanie, 19 Jun 1735 and 31 Jul 1753.

KER, JOHN, late servant to Sir Alexander Burnet of Leys, thereafter residing in Hirl of Crathies, 26 Mar 1757.

KINTRAE, JOHN and MARGARET TAYLOR his wife, in parish of Pitsligo, 20 Jul 1756.

KNIGHT, CHRISTIAN, widow of **Alexander Troup**, late bailie of Old Aberdeen, 4 Dec 1740.

KNOWLES, JOHN, at Miln of Finracy, 16 May 1727 and 25 May 1739.

KNOX, GEORGE, in Seafield, 19 Oct 1736.

KYNOCH, JAMES, merchant in Aberdeen, 3 Jul 1740.

LAFLESH, FRANCIS, merchant in Aberdeen, 27 May 1758.

LAING, JAMES, sometime in Parcock, 1 Dec 1755.

LAMOND, ELSPETH, in Auchindryne, 20 Mar 1756.

LARGOE, ISOBELL, widow of **Alexander Gordon**, bookbinder in Aberdeen, 15 Oct 1747.

LAURENCE, JEAN, widow of **Alexander Bannerman**, town-sergeant of Aberdeen, 28 May 1735.

LAURENSON, ROBERT, in Mid Auchlun, 10 Jun 1743.

LAW, GEORGE, salmon fisher at Bridgend of Don, 5 Jun 1739.

LAW, GEORGE, Mr, sometime Episcopal minister at Aberdeen, 6 Dec 1751.

LAWSON, WILLIAM, weaver in Aberdeen, see **Isobell Cantly**.

LEASK, JOHN, in Muglaw, 27 Dec 1753.

LEASK, WILLIAM, gardener, resident in Aberdeen, 24 Oct 1751.

LEGERTWOOD, ALEXANDER, Mr, sometime in Orchardtoun, late resident in Aberdeen, 5 Jun 1727, 22 Feb 1728 and 25 Nov 1756.

LEGERTWOOD, ELSPETH, lawful daughter of late **William L** of Fornety, 23 Jun 1752.

LEGERTWOOD, JAMES, of Skelmuir, 24 Dec 1756.

LEGERTWOOD, ROBERT, in Northcoulie, 28 Mar 1747.

LEGERTWOOD, WILLIAM, see **Elspeth Legertwood**.

LEGG, JAMES, maltster in Aberdeen. See **Isobell Sey**.

LEGGAT, GEORGE, gardener at Balveny, 12 Sep 1737.

LEITH, GEORGE, in Bodiel, thereafter tin Boghead, 9 Apr 1741.

LEITH, GEORGE, sometime tenant in Boghead, 26 Feb 1739.

LEITH, JOHN, of Leithhall, 13 Aug 1729 and 10 Aug (1736) 1737.

LEITH, MARGARET, widow of Mr **Robert Farquharson**, sometime minister at Kinnethmont, 24 Jan 1758.

LESLIE, ALEXANDER, of Northleslie, 30 May 1749.

LESLIE, ALEXANDER, in Aucherny, brother of **George L**, in Templand of Forgue, 6 May 1751.

LESLIE, ERNEST, of Balquhain, 19 Jun 1740.

LESLIE, GEORGE, see **Alexander Leslie**.

LESLIE, GEORGE, of Northlesslie, 9 Jun 1724 and 7 May 1752.

LESLIE, GEORGE, of Iden, lately residing in Aberdeen, 14 May 1759.

LESLIE, JAMES, of Balquhine, 18 Jan 1732 and 6 May 1735.

LESLIE, JAMES, Mr, of Tullich, 3 Aug and 2 Dec 1731 and 12 Mar 1740.

LESLIE, JAMES, sometime merchant in Aberdeen. See **Janet Ragg**.

LESLIE, JAMES, Mr, sometime minister at St Fergus, 2 Jul 1746, see also **Jean Forbes**.

LESLIE, JEAN, widow of **John Wilson**, shipmaster in Aberdeen, 24 Jun 1743.

LESLIE, JOHN, of Drimmies, see also **Janet Smith**, 22 Jan 1743.

LESLIE, JOHN, of Wartle, 7 Jul 1749.

LESLIE, JOHN, in Tillymadein, parish of Cruden, 18 Dec 1753.

LESLIE, MARGARET, Lady, widow of **Hugh Fraser**, of Kinnairies, 1 May 1744.

LESLIE, NORMAN, in Drumdollo, 4 Mar 1748.

LESLIE, NORMAN, shipmaster in Aberdeen, 20 May 1735.

LESLIE, ROBERT, see **Christian Gordon**.

LESLIE, WILLIAM, Mr, of Littlefolla, 8 Jan 1741.

LEYS, JOHN, merchant in Peterhead, 8 Apr 1736.

LEYS, WILLIAM, in Auchnafoy, 30 Oct 1741.

LEYS, WILLIAM, in Craigley, sometime servant to James Ross in Kirktoun of Birss, 24 Jun 1737.

LILLIE, ALEXANDER, merchant in Old Aberdeen, 18 Aug 1743.

LIND, ALEXANDER, see **Margaret Gow**.

LIND, ALEXANDER, sometime in Seaton of Cairnbulg, 23 Dec 1743.

LINDSAY, JOHN, late bailie in Fraserburgh, 29 Apr 1742.

LITTLEJOHN, ELSPETH, wife to **Robert Craik**, mariner in Aberdeen, 16 Oct 1735.

LITTLEJOHN, PATRICK, sometime merchant in Old Meldrum, 22 Feb 1740 and 16 May 1743.

LIVINGSTON, ALEXANDER, merchant in Aberdeen, 31 Aug 1737.

LIVINGSTON, ANDREW, merchant in Aberdeen, 19 May 1757.

LOGAN, WILLIAM, merchant in Aberdeen, 6 Aug 1753 and 23 May 1754.

LOGIE, ANDREW, merchant in Aberdeen, 29 Jan 1723, 28 Jul 1724 and 7 Aug 1744.

LOGIE, JOHN, in Milenside, 18 Aug 1741.

LOGIE, PATRICK, late in Bamelie, 27 Sep 1737.

LORIMER, WILLIAM, in Dyttach, 30 Apr (1735) 1738 and 9 Aug 1738.

LOW, ALEXANDER, late merchant and shipmaster in Fraserburgh, 15 Sep (19 Nov) 1759.

LOW, WILLIAM, in Kirkhill of Ellon, 27 Feb 1756.

LUMSDEN, CHARLES, sometime dyer, burgess of Aberdeen, 23 May 1737.

LUMSDEN, DAVID, in Auchlossen, 29 Dec 1747.

LUMSDEN, JOHN, watchmaker in Aberdeen, 19 Dec 1751 and 3 Feb 1757.

LUMSDEN, ROBERT, in Burnside of Lumphannan, 16 Jan 1745.

LUMSDEN, THOMAS, of Lyne, and **Marjory Forbes**, his second wife, 7 Jul 1743.

LUMSDEN, WILLIAM, lately mariner in Aberdeen, 21 Nov 1752.

LUNAN, WILLIAM, in Kirktoun of Monymusk, 6 Feb 1736.

LUNDIE, ALEXANDER, see **May Lundie**.

LUNDIE, MAY, lawful daughter of late **Alexander L**, dyer in Aberdeen, 12 Apr and 26 Nov 1736. (Warrant for transmitting her principal testament, etc, 15 Jul 1736).

LYAL, JOHN, only son of the late **John L**, maltster in Aberdeen, 9 Jul 1736.

MCCOMBIE, JAMES, merchant in Aberdeen, 10 Sep 1740 and 19 Mar 1741.

MCCONOCHIE, ISOBELL, widow of **David Couts**, wright in Aberdeen, 6 May 1756.

MCDONALD, DAVID, alias **Guies**, in Spithills of Glenmuick, 1 May 1744.

McGIE, AGNES, daughter of late **John McG**, late surgeon apothecary in Aberdeen, 25 Jun 1756.

MCGIE, JOHN, see **Agnes McGie**.

MCGIE, JOHN, surgeon apothecary in Aberdeen, 13 Jul 1738. See also **Margaret Paterson**.

McHARDIE, ADAM, sometime in Ballach, 2 Jan 1754.

MCHARDIE, CHARLES, of Crathie, 30 Aug 1739 and 28 Dec 1744.

MCHARDIE, FINLAY, sometime in Over Tullochoill, thereafter in Dilvalish, 17 Nov 1757.

MCHARDIE, GEORGE, in Castletown of Curgarf, 3 Dec 1747.

MCHARDIE, JAMES, in Milton of Acholzie, 31 Jan 1755.

MCINTOSH, ELIZABETH, widow of Mr **James Robertson**, minister at Glenmuick, 27 Mar 1756 and 12 Mar 1757.

McKAILL, JAMES, Mr, late minister at Montquhitter, 28 May 1756.

MACKENZIE, DONALD, of Dalmore, 26 May 1749, 13 Mar 1750 and 5 Jan 1751.

MACKENZIE, KENNETH, in Blackwater of St Fergus, 16 Aug 1748.

MACKENZIE, KENNETH, of Dalmore, 26 May 1749.

MACKIE, BARBARA, wife of **James Webster** in Swanfoord, 24 Jul 1740.

MACKIE, GEORGE, shoemaker in Old Meldrum, 8 May 1755.

MACKIE, GEORGE, see **James and George Mackie**.

MACKIE, ISOBELL, widow of **Patrick Wilson**, sometime at Mill of Achry, 8 Oct 1748.

MACKIE, JAMES, in Mains of Auchinhove, 29 Apr 1736.

MACKIE, JAMES, sometime in Kirktoun of Bourtie, 16 Nov 1749.

MACKIE, JAMES, merchant in Portsoy, 18 Nov 1755.

MACKIE, JAMES and GEORGE, merchants in Portsoy, 29 Jun 1756 and 24 Nov 1757.

MACKIE, JOHN, in Mill of Auchleven, 4 Apr 1739 and 1 Dec 1743.

MACKIE, ROBERT, wright in Old Aberdeen, 6 Jun 1751.

MACKIE, THOMAS, in Kirkton of New Deer, 24 Jul 1753.

MACKIE, WILLIAM, in Chapell, in parish of New Machar, 4 Jun 1740.

MACKIE, WILLIAM, sometime in Gooseknows, 24 Mar 1758.

MACLACHLAN, WILLIAM, barber in Cullen, 21 Jul 1743.

MACLAREN, ALEXANDER, late gardener at Seton, 9 Mar 1743.

McPHERSON, DUNCAN, merchant in Banff, 9 Jan 1759.

MCPHERSON, JOHN, sometime in Allanaquich, 10 Feb 1747.

MCPHERSON, ROBERT, in Lachie, parish of Mortlach, 11 Nov 1742.

MCQUEEN, WILLIAM, sometime shopkeeper and resident in Aberdeen, 6 Apr 1738.

MCROBIE, GEORGE, in Finnielost, 8 Jan 1747.

MAIN, ANDREW, shoemaker in Aberdeen, 14 Nov 1754.

MAIR, WILLIAM, sometime in Blackhall, 29 Nov 1754.

MAIR, WILLIAM, Mr, minister at Kincardine O'Neill, see **Barbara Barclay**.

MAITLAND, ELIZABETH, in Fraserburgh, 14 Feb 1740.

MAITLAND, GEORGE, tenant in Fallow, 9 May 1757.

MAITLAND, RICHARD, Mr, minister at Nigg, 11 Nov 1725 and 27 Nov 1740.

MAITLAND, WILLIAM, servant to Alexander Davidson, in Old Bourty, 27 Jan 1743.

MALCOLM, JEAN, in Collonach, 10 Feb 1741.

MALCOLM, MARGARET, wife of **Thomas Shearer**, in Auchmenzie, 8 Sep 1737.

MALCOLM, WILLIAM, in Tilliebirloch, 2 Nov 1727, 23 Jan 1739 and 8 Oct 1754.

MALCOLMSON, JOHN, in Leylodge, 15 Apr 1742.

MAN, ISOBELL, daughter of late **William M**, sometime merchant in Aberdeen, 13 Sep 1759.

MAN, JAMES, at Mill of Aden, 15 Jan 1734 and 27 Jul 1738.

MAN, WILLIAM, see **Isobell Man**.

MARK, FRANCIS, lawful son of late **James M**, merchant in Banff, 13 Dec 1749.

MARK, ISOBELL, wife of **John Duncan**, in Daviot, 14 Jul 1747.

MARK, JAMES, merchant in Banff, 13 Jul 1732 and 25 Jul 1751, see **Francis Mark**.

MARNOCH, JOHN, workman at the Shore of Aberdeen, 30 Mar 1738.

MARNOCH, PATRICK, in Mains of Lenturk, 20 Apr 1739.

MARR, ALEXANDER, butcher, burgess of Aberdeen, 23 Aug 1736.

MARR, DAVID, merchant in Aberdeen, 12 Dec 1743 and 12 Mar 1753.

MARR, GEORGE, merchant in Aberdeen, 23 Sep 1741.

MARR, HELEN, widow of **James Cuming**, merchant in Aberdeen, 9 Apr 1759.

MASSON, JAMES, in Cowfoord, 17 Aug 1738 and 22 Jan 1750.

MASSON, JOHN, merchant in Aberdeen, 27 May 1746.   See also **Barbara Peirie**.

MASSON, JOHN, in Cowfoord, 20 Apr 1750.

MASSON, JOHN, resident in Tarland, 2 Mar (Feb) 1758.

MASSON, WILLIAM, in Lambhill of Fyvie, 24 May 1737.

MASSIE, ALEXANDER, merchant in Aberdeen, 25 Mar 1742.

MATTHEW, CRISTIAN, in Muirtoun of Corse, 1 May 1739.

MAULE, JAMES, at Mill of Kinguidy, 3 Jun 1736 and 15 Mar 1745.

MAWER, GEORGE, in Ferryhill, 30 Aug 1739.

MAWER, JOHN, merchant in Aberdeen, 18 Jul 1739.

MEANIE, JAMES, in Melonside, see **Margaret Dempster**.

MEANIE, ROBERT, in Miltown of Finnersie, 16 Jul 1754.

MEARNS, PETER, merchant in Rayne, 15 May 1738.

MELVILL, ANNA, lawful daughter of Mr **Robert M**, minister at Durris, 30 Oct 1739.

MELVILL, JOHN, Mr, sometime in Hairstonemuir, thereafter in Rammahaggan, 16 Feb 1741.

MELVILL, ROBERT, see **Anna Melvill**.

MELVIN, ELSPETH, widow of **James Harrow**, gardener in Aberdeen, 8 Mar 1750.

MENZIES, ANNE, daughter of the late **Colin M**, merchant in Elgin, 20 Sep 1759.

MENZIES, BARBARA, widow of **William Hay** of Balbithen, 22 Jun 1736.

MENZIES, COLIN, see **Anne Menzies**.

MENZIES, JEAN, Mrs, Lady Auchlunies, 12 Jan 1747.

MERCER, JAMES, see **Anne Irvine**.

MERCER, JEAN, widow of **Thomas Mitchell**, late provost of Aberdeen, 22 Jul 1740.

MERCER, THOMAS, merchant in Aberdeen.   See Mrs **Katharine Arbuthnot**.

MEY, JAMES, in Gateside of Belhelvie, 3 Feb 1742.

MICHIE, ALEXANDER, in Forran, 27 Feb 1740.

MICHIE, CALLUM, in Clashnonie, parish of Towie, son of **Francis M**, in Balgrennie, 4 Dec 1753.
MICHIE, FRANCIS, see **Callum Michie**.
MICHIE, JAMES, at Mill of Rippachie, 13 Jul 1753.
MICHIE, MALCOLM, tailor in Clashnewnie, 24 Apr 1747.
MIDDLETON, ALEXANDER, in Newtoun of Auchlossen, 1 Aug 1740. See also **Anna Cromar**.
MIDDLETON, ALEXANDER, son of **Alexander M**, portioner, sometime of Cannacraig, in parish of Glentanner, sometime resident in Lairg, 8 Dec 1750.
MIDDLETON, ALEXANDER, Capt, late comptroller of Customs at Aberdeen, 4 Jan 1753.
MIDDLETON, GEORGE, Mr, late minister at Keig, 4 Dec 1740.
MIDDLETON, JAMES, sometime in Balnacraig, 10 Mar 1752.
MIDDLETON, JAMES, merchant in Tarves, 11 Oct 1739.
MIDDLETON, JOHN, youngest, merchant in Aberdeen, 21 May 1741.
MIDDLETON, JOHN, of Shiels, sometime Dean of Guild of Aberdeen, 8 Aug 1749.
MILLS, WILLIAM, in Charleton of Aboyne, 26 Jul 1756.
MILNE, ALEXANDER, in Garden, 14 May 1742.
MILNE, DAVID, in Wester Barrack, 2 Dec 1757.
MILNE, GEORGE, in Tipperty, 16 Dec 1743.
MILNE, ISOBEL. See **William Smith**.
MILNE, JAMES, late in Newton of Knockespack, now in Mill of Montgarry. See **Margaret Ingram**.
MILNE, JAMES, tailor, burgess of Aberdeen, 5 Mar 1736.
MILNE, JOHN, merchant, sometime in Wartle, parish of Rain, 8 Feb 1750.
MILNE, JOHN, shipmaster in Banff, 23 Jan 1740.
MILNE, MAGNUS, merchant in Aberdeen, 10 Aug 1737.
MILNE, PETER, in Kincardine O'Neill, 26 Jul 1750.
MILNE, THOMAS, in World's End, 28 Dec 1752.
MILNE, WILLIAM, in Mains of Banchory-Devinick, 2 Aug 1739.
MILNE, ..., mariner and carpenter on board the *St Andrew*, of Aberdeen, 9 May 1758.
MITCHELL, ALEXANDER, tenant in Tilliecorthie, 16 Jul 1742.
MITCHELL, CHRISTIAN, spouse to **John Huie**, in Dummnies, parish of Drumblade, 12 Jul 1740.
MITCHELL, JOHN, in Knowhead of Cromar, 14 Jan 1742.
MITCHELL, JULIAN, sometime in Bogend of Ludquharn, widow of **Andrew Yeat**, sometime in Lennabo, 7 Nov 1751.

MITCHELL, MARGARET, sometime in Kirktoun of St Fergus, widow of **William Steven**, sometime in Blackwater, 20 Apr 1748.

MITCHELL, MARGARET, widow of Mr **John Osburn**, minister at Aberdeen, and Principal of the Marishall College there, 19 Jul 1753.

MITCHELL, ROBERT, woolcomber in Aberdeen, 26 Aug 1756.

MITCHELL, THOMAS, see **Jean Mercer**.

MITCHELL, THOMAS, merchant, and late provost in Aberdeen, and **Thomas M**, late bailie there, his son, 7 Jul 1722, 9 Sep 1726 and 26 Sep 1737.

MITCHELL, WILLIAM, in Wester Tolmads, 21 Mar 1735.

MITCHELL, WILLIAM, wright in Aberdeen, 30 Jul 1744.

MITCHELL, WILLIAM, mariner on board the *Ann* of Aberdeen, 12 Nov 1751.

MITCHELL, WILLIAM, in Millseat of Kingedward, 15 Aug 1753.

MITCHELL, WILLIAM, eldest son of late **William M**, in Balmade, 11 Sep 1756 and 26 Mar 1759.

MOIR, ALEXANDER, in Overhill of Foveran, 27 Nov 1740 and 15 Dec 1743.

MOIR, GEORGE, Mr, minister at Kintore, 10 Jun 1740 and 5 Mar 1741.

MOIR, GILBERT, cooper in Aberdeen, 31 Aug 1742 and 19 Feb 1748.

MOIR, JAMES, in Bochrome, 3 Mar 1752.

MOIR, JEAN, wife of **Alexander Brown** of Nether Asleid, 14 Jul 1740.

MOIR, JOHN, in Tombae, parish of Glenmuick, 29 Nov 1751.

MOIR, JOHN, land surveyor of HM Customs of Aberdeen, 23 Jun 1739.

MOIR, KATHARINE, servant to Alexander Smith of Blairdaff, 23 Dec 1738.

MOIR, ROBERT, in Grayshillock, 1 Jun 1738.

MOIR, ROBERT, sometime in Burnhead of Balvenny, last resident in Lettoch of Murtlack, 14 Jan 1747.

MOIR, WILLIAM, of Invernettie, 22 Dec 1744.

MOIR, WILLIAM, resident in Aberdeen, 19 May 1759.

MOLLISON, ALEXANDER, maltster in Aberdeen, 4 Feb 1752.

MOLLISON, ALEXANDER, of Glascowego, late bailie of Old Aberdeen, 7 Sep 1736.

MOLLISON, JOHN, sometime servant to Mr Horn, in Westhall, 7 Apr 1753.

MOLLISON, ROBERT, in Ardbedie, 5 Feb 1736.

MORE, JAMES, of Stoneywood, see **Jean Abernethy**.

MORGAN, JAMES, see **Robert Morgan**.

MORGAN, MOSES, in Kirktoun of Monymusk, 1 Feb 1749.

MORGAN, PETER, in Bogfairn, 5 Aug 1742.

MORGAN, ROBERT, in Auchmullan, and **James Morgan**, his brother, 28 Aug 1741.

MORISON, ALEXANDER, tailor in Innernorth, 23 Jun 1747.

MORISON, JAMES, senior, late provost of Aberdeen, 1 Feb 1750.

MORISON, JOHN, Mr, in Kirkton of Udny, 19 Feb 1751.

MORTIMER, ELIZABETH, daughter of **James M**, sometime in Tilliechetly, in parish of Alford, 22 Dec 1740.

MORTIMER, JAMES, see **Elizabeth Mortimer**.

MOWAT, ALEXANDER, Mr, minister at Foveran, 9 Jan 1739.

MOWAT, JOHN, of Balquholly, 10 Sep 1747.

MOWAT, JOHN, sometime at Mill of Glentown, in parish of Monymusk, see **Margaret Brownie**.

MOWAT, JOHN, see **Margaret Brownie**.

MOWAT, WILLIAM, maltman in Aberdeen, 8 Apr 1740.

MOWAT, WILLIAM, sometime in Cockstoun, thereafter maltster in Aberdeen, 6 Feb 1736.

MUIRISON, ANDREW, sometime in Mains of Forest, and **Christian Smith**, his wife, 11 Jun 1745.

MULLIGAN, JOHN, see **Isobell Udny**.

MURDOCH, NATHANIEL, in Kirktoun of St Fergus, 8 Dec 1739.

MURRAY, ALEXANDER, sometime in Broomhill, 21 Jul 1749.

MURRAY, DANIEL, merchant in Aberdeen, 18 Jan 1739.

MURRAY, GEORGE, merchant in Old Deer, 12 Aug 1751.

MURRAY, WILLIAM, in Inverichnie, 18 Jul 1753.

MUTCH, JAMES, sometime in Kingsfoord. See **Susan Allan**.

NAIRN, JOHN, sometime in Tarnahaash, 2 Apr 1738.

NICOL, JAMES, merchant and late bailie of Aberdeen, 12 Jan 1750.

NICOL, JOHN, carpenter in Banff, 5 Mar 1742.

NICOL, JOHN, in Greenhall, 15 Dec 1749.

NICOL, THOMAS, in Hillock, parish of Newhills, 11 Feb 1755.

NICOL, WALTER, late merchant in Aberdeen, 11 Aug 1753.

NICOLSON, HELEN, widow of **Andrew Harrow**, mariner in Aberdeen (fragment), 30 Dec 1735.

NICOLSON, JOHN, late in Auchterless. See **Isobel Skene**.

NIDDRY, JOHN, carrier in Old Deer, 23 Apr 1751.

NIDDRY, RACHEL, see **Alexander Booth**.

NOBLE, JAMES, Mr, in Peterhead, 10 Jul 1744.

OGG, WILLIAM, in Over Belnacraig, 21 May 1740.

OGILVIE, ALEXANDER, see **Mary Ogilvie**.

OGILVIE, CORNET WILLIAM, of Bachlaw, 23 Mar (1737) 1738.

OGILVIE, GEORGE, in Braeside of Ludquharn, 27 Nov 1750.

OGILVIE, JAMES, late of Toux. See **Mary Dunbar**.

OGILVIE, JAMES, in Aquhitries, 13 Aug 1745.

OGILVIE, JOHN, of Kempcairn, 23 Jun 1732 and 23 Nov 1742.

OGILVIE, MARY, Mrs, eldest lawful daughter of Sir **Alexander O**, of Forglen, 23 Nov 1738.

OGILVIE, PATRICK, see **Elizabeth Dunbar**.

OGILVIE, ROBERT, of Bachley, 29 Aug 1735.

OGILVIE, THOMAS, dyer in Fraserburgh, 7 Mar 1755. See also **Janet Wemys**.

OGILVIE, WILLIAM, Dr, physician in Banff, 17 Aug 1737.

OGSTON, WILLIAM, senior, tenant in Towie, 28 Aug 1759.

ORD, ALEXANDER, merchant and late bailie of Cullen, 16 Nov 1738.

ORD, JAMES, bailie of Cullen, 4 jUL 1739.

ORD, WILLIAM, sometime in Bogenhilt, 30 Aug 1746.

OREM, ALEXANDER and ANNE, children of late **John O** in Blairdaff, 5 Apr 1742.

OREM, ANNE, see **Alexander Orem**.

OREM, JOHN, see **Alexander Orem**.

OSBURN, JOHN, Mr, minister at Aberdeen and Principal of Marishall College thete. See **Margaret Mitchell**.

PANTON, ADAM, merchant in Banff, 8 Dec 1733 and 24 Sep 1736.

PANTON, ALEXANDER, merchant in Turriff, 19 Aug 1751 and 18 Feb 1752.

PANTON, JAMES, in Burnside of Streichin, 12 Jan 1738.

PANTON, JEAN, in Old Aberdeen, widow of **William Jeans**, merchant there, 12 Dec 1741.

PARK, ANDREW, merchant in Peterhead, 18 Feb 1755.

PARK, JAMES, sometime tenant in Little Byth, 25 Feb 1755.

PARK, JOHN, in Hill of Crimond, 30 May 1754.

PATERSON, ELSPETH, wife of **Andrew Peirie**, in Drumgouan, 22 Feb 1740.

PATERSON, GEORGE, in Lairshill of Fintray, 7 May 1750.

PATERSON, ISOBELL, widow of **Alexander Stewart**, merchant in Aberdeen, 23 Jun 1756.

PATERSON, JAMES, sometime in Little Miln of Leslie, 22 Jan 1754.

PATERSON, JOHN, younger, of Eccles, residing at Counteswells, 30 Sep 1757.

PATERSON, MARY, daughter of late Mr **Robert P**, elder, commissary of Aberdeen, 20 Mar 1753.

PATERSON, ROBERT, see **Mary Paterson**.

PATERSON, WILLIAM, in Hillhead of Bordlam, 13 May 1742.

PATERSON, WILLIAM, merchant in Aberdeen, 2 Apr 1759.

PATON, JOHN, in Mains of Elrick, see **Jean Innes**.

PATON, JOHN, of Grandhome, 3 Apr 1744. See also **Margaret Paton**.

PATON, MARGARET, daughter of late **George P** of Grandholm, 26 Feb 1746.

PAUL, ALEXANDER, in Milntimber, 12 Apr 1757.

PEIRIE, ALEXANDER, sometime in Daviot, 1 Aug 1739.

PEIRIE, ALEXANDER, gardener at Cultur, 19 Mar 1750.

PEIRIE, ANDREW, of Drumgouan, see **Elspeth Paterson**.

PEIRIE, ANDREW, sometime at Mill of Legart, thereafter resident in Aberdeen, 5 Jul 1756.

PEIRIE, GEORGE, in Mudhouse of Foveran, 18 Feb 1749.

PEIRIE, GEORGE, in Quarrieburn, 3 Aug 1759.

PEIRIE, ISOBELL, see **Robert Chalmers**.

PEIRIE, ISOBELL, widow of Mr **Robert Chalmers**, sometime schoolmaster at Turriff, 29 Apr 1735.

PEIRIE, JOHN, in Cotton of Chappelton, 20 Dec 1750.

PEIRIE, JOHN, in Mill of Keithfield, 23 Jan 1735.

PETERKIN, JAMES, late in Woodhead of Fetterletter, 23 Nov 1752.

PETRIE, JOHN, in Bush, parish of Banchory-Ternan, 27 Jul 1742.

PHILP, ALEXANDER, Mr, minister at Boindy, 1 Dec 1743.

PHILP, GEORGE, in Arnhead. See **Anne Smart**.

PHILP, ROBERT, merchant in Buckie, 11 Oct 1736.

PHIN, ALEXANDER, of Auchanacy, 10 Aug 1739.

PIRIE, JOHN, sometime in Mill of Air, thereafter in Mains of Skene, 11 Jun 1745.

PROCTOR, ALEXANDER, in Hillside of Balvenny, 12 Aug 1746 and 3 Feb 1748.

PROCTOR, WILLIAM, late in Rothes, see **Isobell Duffus**.

PYPER, MARGARET, see **Margaret Strachan**.

RAE, ALEXANDER, in Kinaldie, see **Agnes Garden**.

RAE, JAMES, in Maj Gen Stewart's Regiment of Foot in the Dutch Service, 13 Mar 1750.

RAE, WILLIAM, eldest son of George R, portioner in Kintore, 6 Aug 1753.

RAGG, JANET, widow of Mr **James Leslie**, sometime merchant in Aberdeen, 13 Mar 1750.

RAIT, ALEXANDER, Mr, Professor of Philosophy in King's College, Aberdeen, 7 Dec 1751 and 13 Apr 1752.

RAIT, JOHN, sometime portioner of Meikle Follar, 11 Jun 1752.

RAIT, WILLIAM, sometime in Burnside of Kinbrown, 28 Feb 1739 and 21 Dec 1752.

RAMSAY, ARTHUR, merchant in Roseharty, 13 Jul 1743.

REID, ALEXANDER, Capt, younger, of Barra, eldest son of Sir **Alexander Reid** of Barra, 4 Sep 1745.

REID, ALEXANDER, merchant in Aberdeen, 15 Mar 1739.

REID, ALEXANDER, in Auchlie, 17 Feb (1736) 1739.

REID, ANNE, see **William Smith.**

REID, ARTHUR, sometime in Mains of Kildrummie, 26 Jan 1748.

REID, FRANCIS, in Headtown of Meikle Wardhouse, 25 Jun 1745.

REID, GEORGE, Mr, schoolmaster at Banff, 2 mar 1743.

REID, GEORGE, Dr, in Aberdeen, 27 Jun 1755.

REID, JOHN, in Mains of Bodam, 2 Dec 1742.

REID, JOHN, merchant in Aberdeen, 3 Mar 1752.

REID, JOHN, late tenant in Old Keigg, 23 Jun 1752.

REID, JOHN, see **Katharine Reid.**

REID, KATHARINE, daughter of late **John R**, sometime tenant in Spithill, 18 Jun 1756.

REID, WILLIAM, sometime schoolmaster at Leslie, 14 May 1741.

REID, WILLIAM, merchant in Aberdeen, 8 Aug 1749.

RIACH, WILLIAM, in Coldstone, 7 Feb 1749.

RICKART, DAVID, of Rickartoun, see Mrs **Katharine Arbuthnot.**

RICKART, DAVID, see **Janet Rickart.**

RICKART, JANET, Mrs, daughter of late **David R** of Rickarton, 4 Jul 1749 and 7 Mar 1753.

RIDDOCH, GEORGE, in Blairock, and **Elspeth Innes**, his wife, 12 Nov 1751.

RITCHIE, JEAN, late servant of Mrs Taylor, in Aberdeen, 21 Feb 1744.

RITCHIE, JOHN, in Old Keach, 7 Jun 1737.

RITCHIE, KATHARINE, sometime of Marywell, 3 Oct 1751.

RITCHIE, THOMAS, messenger in Aberdeen, 8 Mar 1750.

ROBERTSON, ALEXANDER, senior, merchant in Fraserburgh, 15 Jun 1756.

ROBERTSON, GEORGE, tailor in Muir of Glassaugh, 28 Feb 1758.

ROBERTSON, GILBERT, shipmaster in Peterhead, 14 Aug 1735.

ROBERTSON, ISOBEL and **James Strath**, both in Mossfield, 29 May 1738.

ROBERTSON, JAMES, see **Elizabeth McIntosh.**

ROBERTSON, JANET, sometime in Mosside of Kingswells, thereafter in Cardhillock, widow of **George Smith**, sometime in Broomend, 20 Jan 1756.

ROBERTSON, JOHN, merchant in Cruivie, 18 Jun 1751 and 25 Feb 1752.

ROBERTSON, THOMAS, of Downyhills, 2 Jul 1740, 25 Feb 1741 and 20 Jan 1744.

ROBERTSON, THOMAS, tobacconist in Spittle, 2 Jun 1736.

ROLLAND, ANNE, shopkeeper in Aberdeen, 2 Feb 1742.

ROLLO, JOHN, second son of Robert, Lord Rollo. See Mrs **Mary Kennedy**.

RONALD, JOHN, merchant in Meikle Fintray, 31 Aug 1750.

ROSE, GEORGE, Mr, resident in Mains of Fingask, 8 Jul 1742.

ROSE, MARGARET, Dame, widow of Sir **William Forbes**, of Craigievar, 1 Nov 1740.

ROSE, WALTER, merchant in Aberdeen, 26 Aug 1752.

ROSS, AGNES, widow of **William Touch**, in Kirktoun of Inch, 1 Jun 1748.

ROSS, ALEXANDER, in Forganlachie, 24 Jun 1737.

ROSS, ALEXANDER, at Mill of Kincardine, 29 Dec 1752.

ROSS, ALEXANDER, in Dalwhing, 3 Jan 1753.

ROSS, CHRISTIAN, daughter of late **John R**, sometime merchant in Aberdeen, 4 Feb 1744.

ROSS, CHRISTIAN, Dame, daughter of late **John R**, merchant, and provost of Aberdeen, sometime wife of Sir **Arthur Forbes**, of Craigievar, 28 Sep 1749.

ROSS, FRANCIS, in Mill of Dinnet, and **Hugh R**, his son, 26 Feb 1754.

ROSS, HUGH, see **Francis Ross**.

ROSS, JEAN, in the parish of Kinkell, 5 Jul 1744.

ROSS, JEAN, daughter of late **John R**, merchant in and provost of Aberdeen, and sometime wife to **Alexander Aberdeen**, of Cairnbulg, 28 Sep 1749.

ROSS, JOHN, see **Christian Ross**.

ROSS, JOHN, sometime merchant in Aberdeen, see **Janet Alexander**.

ROSS, WILLIAM, gardener in Aberdeen, 19 Dec 1743.

ROSS, WILLIAM, shipmaster in Aberdeen, 6 Dec 1746.

ROSS, WILLIAM, sometime merchant in Banff, 11 Jul 1751.

RUDDIMAN, JOHN, in Alehouseburn, 11 Aug 1742.

RUDDIMAN, THOMAS, in Sandley, parish of Alva, 24 Nov 1741.

RUGLAN, JAMES, in Kirkhill, 20 Nov 1739.

RUTHERFORD, SOPHIA, widow of .... Smith, in ...... 16 Dec 1737.

SALTON, ALEXANDER, Lord, 9 Apr 1752, 13 Feb and 12 Jul 1753.

SANDERS, DAVID, sometime apothecary in Banff, 31 Jul 1746.

SANG, JOHN, gardener in Ramoir, 22 May 1741.

SANGSTER, GEORGE, tanner in Old Aberdeen, see **Margaret Anderson**.

SCOTT, ALEXANDER, shipmaster in Aberdeen, 2 Jun 1740.

SCROGGIE, ALEXANDER, in Forresterhill, 22 Apr 1746.

SETON, BARBARA, lawful daughter to late **John S**, sometime Dean of Guild of Aberdeen, 23 Nov 1736.

SETON, JAMES, in Scotsmill of Inverugie, 13 Mar 1735.

SETON, JOHN, see **Barbara Seton**.

SETON, ROBERT, at Scotsmill, 21 Jan 1735.

SETON, WILLIAM, Sir, of Pitmeden, Baronet, 26 Jul 1744, 25 Nov 1749, and 15 Aug 1751. See also Dame **Katharine Burnet**.

SEY, ISOBELL, wife of **James Legg**, maltster in Aberdeen, 7 Aug 1751.

SHAND, JAMES, merchant, and late provost of Banff, 21 Jul 1737.

SHAND, JOHN, merchant in Auchmedden, 8 Sep 1735.

SHAND, PATRICK, merchant in Aberdeen, 16 Mar 1720, 5 Dec 1754 and 20 Mar 1749.

SHAND, THOMAS, merchant in Aberdeen, 28 Nov 1748.

SHAND, WILLIAM, merchant in Peterhead, 20 Jul 1751.

SHANK, ALEXANDER, Mr, late minister at Drumoak, 17 Dec 1750.

SHANK, MARTIN, Mr, minister at Upper Banchory, 24 Sep 1747.

SHAW JEAN, in Auchinleith, 14 Sep 1756.

SHAW, JOHN, sometime in Luibmore, 4 Mar 1755.

SHEARER, THOMAS, in Auchmenzie, see **Margaret Malcolm**.

SHEARER, THOMAS, see **Alexander Shearer**.

SHEPHERD, ALEXANDER, ropemaker in Footdee, and late **Barbara Simpson**, his wife, 26 Jan 1750.

SHEPHERD, GEORGE, Mr, sometime minister at Aboyne, 26 Nov 1754.

SHEPHERD, WILLIAM, in Finnon, 1 Dec 1749.

SHERRIFF, ALEXANDER, Mr, writer in Edinburgh, 6 Mar 1741, see **Jean Gordon**.

SHIRRAS, ELIZABETH, resident in Aberdeen, 1 Apr 1745.

SIMPSON, BARBARA, see **Alexander Shepherd**.

SIMPSON, GEORGE, Mr, of Balquhiamachie, 15 Jan 1735.

SIMPSON, JAMES, tailor, and late convener of the Trades of Aberdeen, 9 Jul 1741.

SIMPSON, JANET, widow of **Andrew Smith**, merchant in Peterhead, 24 Aug 1739.

SIMPSON, JEAN, widow of **Alexander Davidson**, merchant in Old Meldrum, 27 Mar and 20 Jun 1735.

SIMPSON, WILLIAM, of Meikle Follow, merchant in Old Meldrum, 8 Jul 1731 and 9 Dec 1742.

SIMPSON, WILLIAM, sometime resident in Oldtown of Carnousey, 23 Jan 1745.

SIMPSON, WILLIAM, Mr, sometime bailie and merchant in Aberdeen, thereafter minister, resident in Fornot, 1 Aug 1749.

SINCLAIR, JAMES, in Malthousecroft, 7 Aug 1746.

SKENE, ALEXANDER, of Dyce, 2 May 1743.

SKENE, ALEXANDER, see **Giles Adie**.

SKENE, ANDREW, of Lethinty, 28 Feb and 15 Mar 1733 and 28 May 1735.

SKENE, ISOBEL, daughter of late James S, merchant in Aberdeen, 12 Jun 1750.

SKENE, JOHN, of Dyce, 3 Dec 1728, 10 Oct 1733 and 26 Feb 1747.

SKENE, MARGARET, widow of **Thomas Finnie**, merchant in Aberdeen, 12 Mar 1750.

SKINNER, ROBERT, landwaiter in Aberdeen, 6 Dec 1759.

SMART, ALEXANDER, in Milnetoun of Lesmurdie, 14 Dec 1737.

SMART, ANNE, last wife to **George Philp**, in Arnhead, 16 Jul 1752.

SMART, ANNE, in Earlsfield, daughter of **Patrick S**, sometime in Pirriesmill, 21 Jun 1753.

SMART, GILBERT, farmer in Aberdeen, 27 Jan 1747.

SMART, JAMES, see **Jean Wilson**.

SMART, PATRICK, see **Anne Smart**.

SMITH, ..., see **Sophia Rutherford**.

SMITH, ADAM, in Mains of Castle Forbes, 19 Dec 1739.

SMITH, ALEXANDER, of Blairdaff, see **Katharine Moir**.

SMITH, ALEXANDER, chapman in Aberdeen, 16 Nov 1749.

SMITH, ALEXANDER, second son of **John S**, in Cortans of Drum, 23 Oct 1755.

SMITH, ALEXANDER, merchant in Aberdeen, 28 Apr 1758.

SMITH, ANDREW, merchant in Peterhead, see **Janet Simpson**.

SMITH, ANN, sometime in Milnbowie. See **James Thomson**.

SMITH, BARTHOLOMEW, sometime papermaker at papermill of Culture, 11 Nov 1758.

SMITH, CHARLES, sometime in Kirkton of Cruden, 21 Nov 1755.

SMITH, CHRISTIAN, see **Andrew Muirison**.

SMITH, GEORGE, see **Janet Robertson**.

SMITH, GILBERT, in Ord, and **Robert S**, in Drummoack, 24 Jun 1730 and 30 Nov 1750.

SMITH, JAMES, in Tilfogger, 4 Mar 1748.

SMITH, JAMES, blacksmith in Cullen, 18 May 1739.

SMITH, JAMES, farmer at Woolmanhill of Aberdeen, 8 Nov 1758.

SMITH, JANET, widow of **John Leslie**, of Drimmies, 19 Jul 1748.

SMITH, JOHN, see **Alexander Smith**.

SMITH, JOHN, merchant in Aberdeen, see **Jean Weir**.

SMITH, JOHN, sometime in Christ's Kirk, 19 Jun 1750.

SMITH, JOHN, see **Alexander Smith**.

SMITH, MARJORY, resident in Aberdeen, sometime servant to Lady Cairnfield, 30 Nov 1738.

SMITH, MARY, see **Alexander Cruickshank**.

SMITH, PATRICK, in Kirktoun of Alva, 8 Nov 1743.

SMITH, PETER, in Newkirk of Coldstone, 23 Jul 1736.

SMITH, ROBERT, in the land of Kingswells, 17 Jan 1743.

SMITH, ROBERT, see **Gilbert Smith**.

SMITH, WILLIAM, merchant in Aberdeen, and **Anne Reid**, his wife, 24 Jun 1751.

SMITH, WILLIAM, in Little Finracy, 11 Aug 1739.

SMITH, WILLIAM, merchant in Aberdeen, and **Isobel Milne**, his wife, 26 Feb 1753.

SMITH, WILLIAM, see **Mary Cruickshank**.

SOUPER, WILLIAM, merchant in Aberdeen, 30 Jun 1725 and 11 Dec 1745, see also **Jean Byers**.

SPEEDIMAN, DAVID, glover, burgess of Aberdeen.   See **Christian Adamson**.

SPENCE, ELSPET, see **William Ingram**.

SPENCE, FRANCIS, see **William Ingram**.

SPENCE, JAMES, porter at Kiethhall, 23 Dec 1755.

SPENCE, JOHN, late servant to the Laird of Invercauld, 5 Feb 1741.

STABLES, CHRISTIAN, see **Helen Stables**.

STABLES, HELEN and CHRISTIAN, in Charleston of Aboyne, 4 Mar 1755.

STEPHEN, ELIZABETH, daughter of late **John S** portioner in Inverury, 5 Dec 1744.

STEPHEN, GEORGE, sometime in Bruckles, parish of Auchterless, 30 Nov 1742.

STEPHEN, GEORGE, see **James Stephen**.

STEPHEN, JAMES, only son of late **George S**, in Bruckles, parish of Auchterless, 3 Jul 1755.

STEPHEN, JAMES, in Cullen, 17 Oct 1740.

STEPHEN, JEAN, resident in Aberdeen, 14 Aug 1735.

STEPHEN, JOHN, see **Elizabeth Stephen**.

STEPHEN, JOHN, in Headtoun of Meikle Wardhouse, 13 Sep 1751.

STEPHEN, JOSEPH, merchant in Daviot, 4 Jun 1748.

STEPHEN, THOMAS, in Little Wartle, 7 Dec 1749.

STEPHEN, WILLIAM, sometime in Blackwater, see **Margaret Mitchell**.

STEPHEN, WILLIAM, shoemaker in Old Meldrum, 22 Jul 1737.

STEPHENSON, ALEXANDER, see **Barbara Stephenson**.

STEPHENSON, BARBARA, lawful daughter of the late **Alexander S**, sometime gardener at Mounie, 7 Feb 1740.

STEVENSON, GEORGE, see **Isobell Davidson**.

STEVENSON, ISOBELL, daughter of **John S**, apothecary in Banff, 2 Jun 1748.

STEVENSON, JOHN, see **Isobell Stevenson**.

STEWART, ALEXANDER, merchant in Aberdeen, 8 Jan 1736, see also **Isobel Paterson**.

STEWART, ALEXANDER, sometime of Lesmurdie, see **Magdalen Crichton**.

STEWART, ALEXANDER, servant at Slains, 29 Jun 1757.

STEWART, ALEXANDER, of Auchoillie, 5 Jun 1746, 14 May 1747 and 27 Sep 1748.

STEWART, ALEXANDER, sometimes of Lesmurdie, see **Magdalen Crichton**.

STEWART, CHARLES, late in Pittenbringen, 7 Jun 1750 and 2 May 1753.

STEWART, DAVID, supervisor of Excise in Aberdeen, 20 Apr 1748.

STEWART, GEORGE, of Tannachie, 6 Jul 1749 and 26 Jul 1750.

STEWART, JAMES, merchant in Cullen, 10 Oct 1746.

STEWART, JAMES, in Blackhill of Oxhill, 17 Apr 1752.

STEWART, JEAN, widow of **Andrew Cassie**, sometime Town Clerk of Old Aberdeen, 21 Jun 1756.

STEWART, JOHN, of Balleatrich, sometime factor to Earl of Aboyne, 26 Jul 1726 and 15 Aug 1740.

STEWART, JOHN, Mr, minister at Drumblade, 13 Dec 1744.

STEWART, MARGARET, sometime widow to late **William Farquharson**, in Millhead of Melgin, thereafter wife of **Alexander Grant**, now in Glencarvie, 24 Feb 1755.

STEWART, ROBERT, merchant, and sometime provost of Banff, 24 Feb 1747 and 15 Feb 1757.

STEWART, ROBERT, merchant, and late provost of Aberdeen, 12 Mar 1752 and 23 Apr 1753.

STEWART, WILLIAM, maltster in Aberdeen, 16 Jun 1744.

STICHELL, JOHN, late in Denside of Farsken, 21 Dec 1752.

STILL, ALEXANDER, sometime in Murcar. See **Christian Watson**.

STILL, DOROTHEA, sometime resident in Aberdeen, 17 Feb 1759.

STILL, JOHN, sometime farmer in Cotton, 23 Jun 1747 and 12 Jan 1749, see also **Isobell Duncan**.

STIRLING, GILBERT, Mr, sometime schoolmaster at Cruden, 3 Jul 1745.

STIRLING, GILBERT, in Auchmadie, 2 May 1747.

STIRRET, DAVID, in Glassell, 20 Jun 1735.

STRACHAN, ALEXANDER, son of **Robert S**, of Tillieriach, see **Marjory Garrioch**.

STRACHAN, ALEXANDER, of Dalhakie, 18 May 1739 and 30 Jul 1741.

STRACHAN, ALEXANDER, in Mill of Auchleven, 17 Mar 1756.

STRACHAN, ANNE, see **John Strachan**.

STRACHAN, JOHN, merchant and late bailie of Aberdeen, and **Anne S**, his sister, children of **John S**, sometime of Kincardine, 12 Dec 1749.

STRACHAN, JOHN, senior, merchant in Aberdeen, 19 Dec 1735.

STRACHAN, JOHN, see **William Strachan**.

STRACHAN, MARGARET, alias **Pyper**, widow of **John S**, merchant and late bailie of Aberdeen, 5 Dec 1749.

STRACHAN, MARGARET, see **Thomas Strachan**.

STRACHAN, ROBERT, Mr, see **Marjory Garrioch**.

STRACHAN, THOMAS, merchant and late bailie of Aberdeen, and **Margaret S**, his daughter, 13 Dec 1738.

STRACHAN, WILLIAM, merchant in Aberdeen, 2 Jun and 23 Nov 1747.

STRACHAN, WILLIAM, in Inaltrie, and **John S**, there, his son, 26 Mar 1751.

STRATH, JAMES, in Mossfield, see **Isobel Robertson**.

STRATH, WILLIAM, in Denhead of Knaven, 28 Dec 1752.

SUTHERLAND, CHARLES, late soldier in Regiment of NB Grey Dragoons, commanded by Lt Gen John, Earl of Rothes, 20 Nov 1753.

SYM, WILLIAM, see **Jean Davie**.

SYME, JOHN, Mr, sometime minister at Loanmay, 28 Dec 1752.

SYME, WILLIAM, sometime merchant and bailie of Banff, see **Jean Davie**.

SYMMER, THOMAS, Lt of HM Navy, sometime residing in Aberdeen, thereafter at Faichfield, 28 Jul (Aug) 1755.

TAES, JOHN, merchant in Banff, 10 Feb 1747.

TARRAS, JAMES, merchant in Portsoy, 2 Mar 1744 and 11 May 1748.

TAYLOR, JAMES, sometime in Orchens, 15 Feb 1753.

TAYLOR, JAMES, in Buntin Bush, 7 Dec 1738.

TAYLOR, JOHN, in Meikleesie, 11 Jan 1738.

TAYLOR, JOHN, in Overside, 9 Mar 1742.

TAYLOR, JOHN, Mr, late schoolmaster at Keig, 11 May 1754.

TAYLOR, JOHN, late shipbuilder in Peterhead, 27 Jan 1757.

TAYLOR, MARGARET, see **John Kintrae**.

TAYLOR, ROBERT, in Tarves, 12 Apr 1756.

TAYLOR, THOMAS, in Auchleven, and **Margaret Innes**, his wife, 8 Aug 1758.

TAYLOR, WILLIAM, in Easter Edieston, 4 Oct 1749.

TENNANT, MARGARET, in Mill of Pitdavie, parish of Boundie, 29 May 1755.

THAIN, WILLIAM, Mr, of Blackhall, 2 Feb 1736, see **Elizabeth Thain**, and also **Marjory Davidson**.

THOM, JOHN, in Pitmarchie, 15 Dec 1741.

THOMSON, ALEXANDER, farmer in Aberdeen, 12 Jul 1746.

THOMSON, ALEXANDER, Mr, of Portlethen, Town-Clerk of Aberdeen, 29 Oct 1729, 29 Oct 1730, 11 Feb 1735 and 15 Nov 1739.

THOMSON, ANDREW, in Portleithen, 4 Aug 1743.

THOMSON, ANDREW, merchant in Aberdeen, 1 Sep 1757.

THOMSON, CHRISTIAN, see **Gilbert Davidson**.

THOMSON, ELIZABETH, wife to **James Gellie**, sometime tide surveyor, now land surveyor of HM Customs at Aberdeen, 12 Jul 1744.

THOMSON, ELIZABETH, daughter of **William T**, at Newmill of Logie, 16 Aug 1748.

THOMSON, ELIZABETH, widow of Mr **Robert Burnet**, minister at Newhills, 17 May 1737.

THOMSON, ISOBELL, see **John Clark**.

THOMSON, JEAN, see **Alexander Bain**.

THOMSON, ROBERT, shoemaker in Hattown of Fintray, 5 Oct 1739.

THOMSON, PETER, in Ley of Drumalachie, 31 Jan 1753.

THOMSON, WILLIAM, see **Elizabeth Thomson**.

THOMSON, WILLIAM, merchant in Aberdeen, see also **Jean Couts**, 7 May 1735.

THOMSON, WILLIAM, in Mill of Legatt, 22 Apr 1748.

TIBO, ELIZABETH, late of the precinct of Haxton, County Middlesex, but late of Aberdeen, 17 Feb 1756.

TOLMIE, PETER, shipmaster in Aberdeen, 12 Nov 1754.

TORN, JAMES, in Old Meldrum, and **Jean Anderson**, his wife, 22 Jun 1749.

TOSH, ALEXANDER, Mr, minister at Tarland, and **Margaret Gordon**, his wife, 23 Jun 1737.

TOUCH, WILLIAM, see **Agnes Ross**.

TRAILL, JOHN, gardener in Aberdeen, See **Margaret Massie**.

TROUP, ALEXANDER, late bailie of Old Aberdeen, see **Christian Knight**.

TURING, JOHN, Mr, minister at Drumblade, 24 Dec 1735 and 5 Feb 1742.

TURING, WALTER, Mr, minister at Rain, 12 Mar 1746.

TURRIFF, JAMES, merchant in Old Aberdeen, 5 Jun 1740.

TWEED, GEORGE, sometime in Milntoun of Fishery, 19 Aug 1747.

TYRIE, ANNE, eldest daughter of David T. of Dunideer, 26 Dec 1751.

TYRIE, DAVID, of Dunideer, 22 Dec 1750.

TYTLER, JAMES, elder, at Mill of Corsinday, 12 Apr 1754.

UDNY, ISOBELL, widow of Mr **John Mulligan**, minister at Methlick, 14 Jun 1744.

UDNY, ISOBELL, wife of **Alexander Gordon** of Barrack, 27 Feb 1736.

URQUHART, GEORGE, vintner and merchant in Turriff, 19 Jun 1755.

URQUHART, JAMES, merchant or chapman in Ghamery, 20 Jan 1744.

URQUHART, JOHN, of Meldrum, 11 Feb 1727 and 10 Feb 1735.

URQUHART, MARY, Mrs, daughter of **William U** of Meldrum, 24 Jul 1759.

URQUHART, WILLIAM, late of Whitehill, 30 Jun 1742.

URQUHART, WILLIAM, merchant in Turriff, sometime travelling chapman and residing in Aberdeen, 29 Jan 1751.

URQUHART, WILLIAM, see **Mary Urquhart**.

VERNOR, DAVID, Mr, late Professor of Philosophy in Marishall College, Aberdeen, 17 Jul 1752.

WALKER, ALEXANDER, in the Meikletoun of Slains, 15 Feb 1735.

WALKER, ALEXANDER, late provost of Aberdeen, see **Helen Irvine**.

WALKER, ALEXANDER, in Mill of Keithhall, 13 Jun 1752.

WALKER, ALEXANDER, see **John Walker**.

WALKER, HELEN, resident in Aberdeen, 12 Jun 1750.

WALKER, JAMES, Commissary clerk-depute of Aberdeen, 12 ALpr 1738 and 8 Jan 1747.

WALKER, JOHN, sometime in Ardmurdo, 12 Sep 1755.

WALKER, WILLIAM, merchant in Aberdeen, 22 Feb 1739.

WALLACE, JOHN, sometime in Cookstone, 10 May 1738.

WALLACE, THOMAS, sailor in Aberdeen, 8 Jun 1751.

WATSON, CHRISTIAN, widow of **Alexander Still**, sometime in Murcar, 10 Nov 1750.

WATSON, GEORGE, in Walkmill, in lands of Parkhill, 24 Jul 1742.

WATSON, GEORGE, in Cults, son of **George W**, there, 12 Aug 1742.

WATSON, JANET, in parish of Longside, 24 Jul 1750.

WATT, JAMES, in Raithen, 4 Jul 1752.

WATT, JOHN, see **Margaret Anderson**.

WEBSTER, JAMES, in Swanfoord, see **Barbara Mackie**.

WEBSTER, JOHN, Mr, minister, sometime at New Deer, thereafter at Cruden, 29 Mar 1743 and 23 Jul 1752.

WEIR, JEAN, widow of **John Smith**, merchant in Aberdeen, 18 Aug 1737.

WEMYSS, GEORGE, sometime in Little Boghead, 13 Apr 1749.

WEMYSS, JANET, widow of **Thomas Ogilvie**, dyer in Fraserburgh, 7 Feb 1737.

WEMYSS, JOHN, late tacksman of the Mains of Aberdour, 6 Jan 1749.

WEMYSS, WILLIAM, of Craighall, 7 Oct 1746.

WHITE, GEORGE, in Bogside of Auchterless, 20 Feb 1755.

WHITE, WILLIAM, sometime treasurer and burgess of Cullen, 6 Oct 1737.

WIDOWSON, JAMES, in Fiddesbegg, 29 May 1735.

WIGHT, ADAM, in Nethertoun of Balquhain, 2 Nov 1750.

WILDGOOSE, JOHN, in Braehead of Auchtidonald, 21 Jun 1759.

WILL, ALEXANDER, tenant in Badifash, 2 Dec 1746.

WILLOX, JAMES, merchant in Turriff, 20 Jan 1748.

WILSON, ALEXANDER, see **Jean Alexander**.

WILSON, ANDREW, sometime at Rhannis, see **Anne Hilton**.

WILSON, DAVID, of Finzeauch, 8 Feb 1735.

WILSON, JAMES, see **Mary Wilson**.

WILSON, JAMES, Mr, late schoolmaster at Banchory-Ternan, 16 May 1740.

WILSON, JEAN, widow of **James Smart**, at Mill of Willimastoun, 2 Dec 1742.

WILSON, JEAN, sister-german of late **Alexander W** of Littlefield, 17 May 1745.

WILSON, JOHN, sometime in Formeston of Aboyne, 24 Dec 1746.

WILSON, JOHN, shoemaker at Well of Spaw, 22 May 1758.

WILSON, JOHN, see **Jean Leslie**.

WILSON, MARY, resident in Aberdeen, widow of **James W**, clerk to Mr Drummond, banker at Charing Cross, London, 3 Oct 1738.

WILSON, PATRICK, sometime at Mill of Achry, see **Isobell Mackie**.

WILSON, PETER, servant to **William Wilson**, in Seats of Touch, 19 Jun 1746.

WILSON, THOMAS, advocate in Aberdeen, 16 Jun 1748 and 16 May 1758.

WISHART, JAMES, merchant in Aberdeen, 29 May 1742.

WOOD, ALEXANDER, sailor in Portsoy, 18 Jan 1743.

WOOD, ALEXANDER, mariner in Aberdeen, son of **Charles W**, wright in Pitmuckstoun, 28 Jun 1750.

WOOD, CHARLES, see **Alexander Wood**.

WOOD, JAMES, writer and messenger in Banff, 26 Jul 1743.

WOOD, JOHN, chapman in Ellon, 4 Aug 1744.

WOOD, WILLIAM, shoemaker in Roseharty, 11 Nov 1742 and 17 Jan 1745.

WYNHOUSE, JAMES, in Cortans, 27 Jan 1726 and 27 Mar 1739.

YEAT, ANDREW, sometime in Leunabo, see **Julian Mitchell**.

YOUNG, JAMES, sometime surgeon in Ellon, 25 May 1749.

YOUNG, JOHN, in Balmoral, 20 Jan 1736.

REGISTER OF TESTAMENTS

ABERDEEN

Part Three: 1760-1800

INTRODUCTION

Some of the most important sources of information on our ancestors are to be found in the form of testaments. These documents can be expected to reveal the name and designation of the deceased, normally the date of death, the executor, an inventory of assets, liabilities, debtors and creditors, and usually a will. Registers of Testaments are generally available from the late 16th century to the early 19th century, and these contain significant material of relevance to the family historian. It should, however, be noted that not everyone left a will, and of those made, not all found their way into the books of the Commissary Court.

Until the 1820s, testaments in Scotland were "confirmed", by various Commissariot Courts throughout the land. These Courts were based roughly on pre-Reformation dioceses boundaries. The Commissariot Court of Edinburgh was often used by Scots residing overseas. After the 1820s documents were usually, but not exclusively, lodged in the local Sheriff Court, with Edinburgh continuing to be used by those living abroad.

Fire destroyed the early records of the Commisariot of Aberdeen, including testaments, and the surviving records date only from 1715. This publication is in essence an alphabetical listing of the testaments confirmed by the Commissary Court of Aberdeen for the period 1760 to 1800.

St Andrews
1997

iii

REGISTER OF TESTAMENTS
ABERDEEN
1760-1800

ABELL, JAMES, in Aquerthen, parish of Kintore, 26 Nov 1776 and 7 Dec 1776.

ABERCROMBIE, BESSIE, widow of Dr **James Hay**, sometime minister of Elgin, who resided in Aberdeen, 21 Sept 1790.

ABERCROMBIE, GEORGE, Mr, one of the ministers of Aberdeen, 29 Apr 1791. See also **Jean Leslie**.

ABERCROMBIE, JAMES, see **Elspet Ord**.

ABERCROMBIE, JOHN, merchant, late baillie of Aberdeen, 16 Dec 1789.

ABERDEEN, ALEXANDER, land measurer, son of **Alexander A**, gardener at Auchiries, 15 Nov 1765.

ABERDEEN, ALEXANDER, of Cairnbulg, 30 May 1768. See also **Jean Ross**.

ABERDEEN, WILLIAM, Earl of, 6 and 27 Jun 1745, 18 Jul 1759, 21 Jun 1760.

ABERNETHY, ALEXANDER, merchant in Aberdeen, 18 May 1796.

ABERNETHY, WILLIAM, late of Crimonmogate, 11 Oct 1793.

ADAM, Alexander, flax-dresser in Aberdeen, 11 Nov 1794.

ADAM, ALEXANDER, sometime merchant in Elgin, thereafter residing in Aberdeen, 14 Sept 1799.

ADAM, JOHN, at Manse of Cushnie, 21 Jul 1797.

ADAMSON, ALEXANDER, in Collegeford, 10 Sept 1795.

ADAMSON, JAMES, mariner and whitefisher in Whitehills, 8 Jul 1784.

ADIELL, WILLIAM, wright in Broadland, 21 Nov 1769.

AIKEN, JAMES, see **Isabell Hector**.

AITKINE, WILLIAM, residing at Denburn of Aberdeen, 27 Sept 1791.

ALEXANDER, ANN, late in Muirden, parish of Alva, 28 Jul 1790.

ALEXANDER, GEORGE, sometime merchant in Aberdeen, 22 Apr 1784.

ALEXANDER, GEORGE, merchant in Aberdeen, and **Janet Henry**, his spouse, 28 Jul 1786.

ALEXANDER, JAMES, see **Helen Gordon**.

ALEXANDER, JEAN, see **George Gray**.

ALEXANDER, PETER, wright in Mill of Cathie, 5 Mar 1790.

ALEXANDER, WILLIAM, late of Mains of Barra, 6 Oct 1763.

1

ALLAN, COLIN, late goldsmith in Aberdeen, 17 Jul 1777.

ALLAN, ELIZABETH, widow of **Andrew Wylie**, barber in Aberdeen, 22 May 1800.

ALLAN, GEORGE, baker in Aberdeen, 28 Jan 1783.

ALLAN, JAMES, merchant in Aberdeen, 15 Nov 1769. See **Janet Miller**.

ALLAN, JAMES, in Wester-Earlseat, 15 Nov 1769.

ALLAN, JAMES, merchant in Aberdeen, 21 Nov 1782.

ALLAN, JAMES, merchant in Buckie, 7 May 1788.

ALLAN, JANET, widow of **William Cattanach**, residenter in Aberdeen, 12 May 1784.

ALLAN, JEAN, sometime at Whitehaugh, thereafter residing in Aberdeen, 25 Mar 1789.

ALLAN, JEAN, wife of **Alexander Davidson**, merchant in Aberdeen, 15 May 1793.

ALLAN, JOHN, sometime in Dorsinsilly, 12 Mar 1794 and 22 Jun 1795. See **Elspeth Elmsly**.

ALLAN, ROBERT, of Caldwells, merchant in Aberdeen, 12 Mar 1794 and 22 Jun 1795.

ALLARDICE (ALLARDES), JAMES, merchant in Aberdeen, 7 Jan 1779 and 2 and 26 Feb 1780.

ALLARDICE, WILLIAM, sometime in Corbshill, parish of New Deer, 23 Jan 1784.

ANDERSON, ALEXANDER, in Abbey of Deer, 8 Jun 1762.

ANDERSON, ALEXANDER, shoemaker at Denburn, in Gilcomston, 18 Jul 1771.

ANDERSON, ALEXANDER, late of Customhouse boat at the Port of Aberdeen, 23 Jul 1789.

ANDERSON, BASIL, Mr, minister at Old Deer, 12 Feb 1798.

ANDERSON, CHRISTIAN, residing in Aberdeen, widow of **William Ellison**, mariner on board the *Millford* man o war, 4 Mar 1783.

ANDERSON, CHRISTIANA, widow of **William Finnie**, wright in Aberdeen, 29 Jul 1800.

ANDERSON, GEORGE, merchant in Newton of Clatt, 16 Feb 1797.

ANDERSON, ISOBELL, widow of **Thomas Milne**, sometime in Auchiries, 16 Jul (Aug) 1760.

ANDERSON, ISOBELL, daughter of **Patrick A**, of Bourtie, 30 Jul 1768.

ANDERSON, JAMES, late of Whittlesea, thereafter residing in Aberdeen, 20 Aug 1793.

ANDERSON, JEAN, widow of **Robert Brebner**, resident in Buckie, 14 Nov 1775.

ANDERSON, JEAN, resident in Aberdeen, 6 Dec 1780.

ANDERSON, JEAN, daughter of late **Patrick A** of Bourtie, 19 Jul 1781.

ANDERSON, JOHN, sometime in Ruthven in Cromar, thereafter in Cottmore, 24 Aug 1786.

ANDERSON, PATRICK, of Bourtie, pewterer in Aberdeen, 27 Jul 1764.

ANDERSON, RACHEL, daughter of **Patrick A**, of Bourtie, 30 Jul 1768.

ANDERSON, WILLIAM, cooper at Rayne, 16 Sept 1776.

ANDERSON, WILLIAM, merchant in Cullen, 16 Apr 1781.

ANGUS, HELEN, daughter of late **William A**, merchant in Aberdeen, 29 Oct 1779.

ANGUS, THOMAS, merchant in Aberdeen, 29 Oct 1779.

ANNAND, ISOBELL, in Ellon, 27 Jun 1774.

ANNAND, JANET, see **William George**.

ARBUTHNOT, ANN, fourth daughter of **James A**, merchant in Peterhead, 11 May 1791.

ARBUTHNOT, CHRISTIAN, Miss, in Kirktoun of Peterhead, daughter of late **James A,** in Rora, 31 Dec 1796.

ARBUTHNOT, ELIZABETH, eldest daughter of the late **John A**, of Fordoun, 23 Feb 1768.

ARBUTHNOT, JOHN, white thread manufacturer in Peterhead, second son of **James A**, merchant there, 11 May 1791.

ARBUTHNOT, KATHARINE, widow of **James Moir** of Invernetty, Esq, 4 Apr 1775.

ARBUTHNOT, MAY, Mrs, widow of **William Dunbar**, of Grant, Esq, 20 Jan 1779.

ARBUTHNOT, THOMAS, shipmaster in Peterhead, 7 Jan 1780.

ARBUTHNOT, THOMAS, late merchant in Peterhead, 6 Jan 1794.

AULDJO, JOHN, of Portlethen, 20 Feb 1787.

BAGRA, JEAN, widow of **John Brodie**, late mason in Portsoy, 17 Mar 1791.

BALFOUR, ALEXANDER, merchant in Aberdeen, 29 Apr 1799.

BALFOUR, GEORGE, late merchant in Old Aberdeen, 15 Jul 1790.

BALFOUR, SYLVESTER, late in Littlemains of Clackruach, 31 Jan 1785.

BALLINGALL, WILLIAM, Mr, schoolmaster in Old Aberdeen, 15 Apr 1769.

BANNERMAN, EDWARD TROTTER, Sir, Bart, lately residing at Kincardine Lodge, 28 Jan 1797.

BARCLAY, ANDREW, in Broadlyhill, parish of Slains, 6 Aug 1782.

BARCLAY, JOHN, see **Anne Gordon**.

BARRACK, WILLIAM, in Ellon, 14 Feb 1760.

BARRON, PATRICK, of Woodside, merchant in Aberdeen, 26 Jun 1800.

BARRON, PETER, late in Cruivehead, parish of Meldrum, 13 Dec 1774.

BARTLET, ELIZABETH, widow of **Alexander Martin**, maltster in Aberdeen, 18 Mar 1780.

BARTLET, GEORGE, sometime merchant and wigmaker in London, thereafter residing in Aberdeen, 3 Feb 1797.

BARTLET, GEORGE, Mr, minister at Old Aberdeen, 30 Jul 1771.

BARTLET, JAMES, late in Gardenstoun, 12 Aug 1800.

BARTLET, JOHN, tenant at Walkmiln of Parkhill, 3 Dec 1761.

BAXTER, ALEXANDER, of Glassell, 22 May 1758.

BAXTER, ANDREW, late shipmaster in Aberdeen, 13 May 1779.

BAXTER, ROBERT, in Fetterletter, 2 Oct 1764.

BAXTER, ROBERT, late in Ardlogie, 22 Mar 1782.

BEAN, JOHN, shoemaker at Gilcomstone, near Aberdeen, 19 Jun 1781.

BEAN, JOHN, late of London, thereafter residing at Denburn, near Aberdeen, and **Christian Cooper**, his wife, 19 Jul 1799.

BEATON, JAMES, in Gardenend of Saak of Deer, 23 Mar 1778.

BEATTIE, JEAN, wife of **Patrick Gall**, in Foggyrigg, 7 Oct 1784.

BEET, WILLIAM, blacksmith in Aberdeen, see **Elizabeth Hay.**

BEGG, GEORGE, sometime in Drumgask, thereafter in Auchinhove, 6 Mar 1775.

BEGG, LUCRETIA, widow of **Alexander Millison**, late maltman, burgess in Aberdeen, 26 Jun 1777.

BENNET, WILLIAM, in Fortree, 4 Nov 1800.

BEVERLY, JAMES, see **Isobell Still**.

BEVERLY, MARGARET, widow of **Robert Reid**, farmer in Dub Castle, 12 Oct 1775.

BIRNIE, JAMES, farmer in Aberdeen, 28 Dec 1788.

BIRNIE, JAMES, sometime planter in Tobago, afterwards in Techmuiry, 11 Aug 1799.

BIRNIE, MOSES, late merchant in Aberdeen, 25 May 1797.

BIRNIE, PETER, late at Mill of Milldurno, 10 Jun 1791.

BIRNIE, SAMUEL, merchant in Fraserburgh, 12 Mar 1763.

BIRNIE, WILLIAM, shipmaster in Peterhead, 23 Jan 1788.

BIRNIE, WILLIAM, sometime in Overtoun of Straloch, 20 Aug 1794.

BLACK, ALEXANDER, see **Jean Stephen**.

BLACK, ALEXANDER, in Memeula, parish of Newmachar, 31 Jan 1763.

BLACK, JAMES, officer of Excise at Newburgh, brother-german of late **William B**, junior, writer in Dunfermline, 29 Sept 1774.

BLACK, PATRICK, Mr, minister at Peterculter, 15 Jun 1767.

BLYTH, CHRISTIAN, residing in Old Aberdeen, 16 Jul 1790.

BOOKER, THOMAS, see Lady **Katherine Gordon**.

BOSWELL, ANN, widow of **John Fleming**, weaver in Aberdeen, 20 Jul 1784.

BOTHWELL, WILLIAM, sometime merchant in Old Meldrum, 3 Mar 1785.

BOWMAN, JAMES, in Clachanturn, 26 Jan 1790.

BOYN, JAMES, Excise Officer in Aberdeen, 23 Feb 1790.

BRAND, ROBERT, carver in Aberdeen, 29 Jan 1778.

BREBNER, ALEXANDER, shipmaster in Aberdeen, 16 Jun 1800.

BREBNER, ALEXANDER, surgeon, resident in Aberdeen, 23 Feb 1762.

BREBNER, GEORGE, in Tullo, parish of Old Meldrum, 6 Nov 1782.

BREBNER, JAMES, merchant in Aberdeen. See **Ann Mason**, 25 Mar 1784.

BREBNER, JEAN, widow of **Andrew Dyce**, shipmaster in Aberdeen, 25 Mar 1784.

BREBNER, ROBERT, see **Jean Anderson**.

BREBNER, ROBERT, see **Barbara Shirras**.

BRECK, JEAN, see **William Burnet**.

BRICK, JOSEPH, wright in Tollohill, 9 Mar 1790.

BRISBANE, JOHN, see **Grizel Ogilvie**.

BRITTON, PEMBER, Capt. See **Margaret Milne**.

BRODIE, JOHN, shipmaster in Peterhead, 19 Aug 1772.

BRODIE, JOHN, late mason in Portsoy. See **Bagra, Jean**, 1791.

BROWN, ALEXANDER, of Ashleid, 23 Jun 1769.

BROWN, DUNCAN, in Graystone, 17 Jul 1789.

BROWN, JAMES, sometime merchant in Portsoy, 24 Mar 1792.

BROWN, JOHN, in Laichie, 16 Jul 1760.

BRUCE, ALEXANDER, wright in Auchlin, parish of Aberdour, 5 Dec 1765.

BRUCE, ALEXANDER, merchant in Banff, 13 Dec 1781.

BRUCE, ALEXANDER, merchant in Gardesntoun, 13 Nov 1794(1793).

BRUCE, GEORGE, coal merchant in Aberdeen, 1 Jul 1783, 7 and 12 Feb 1784.

BRUCE, WILLIAM, late in Milltoun of Savock, 28 Feb 1774.

BRUCE, WILLIAM, sailor in Aberdeen, 4 May 1787.

BURNET, ANN, Mrs, widow of Dr **John Gordon**, sometime minister of St Paul's Chapel, Aberdeen, 15 Oct 1791.

BURNET, CHRISTIAN, widow of **William Durward**, merchant, burgess of Aberdeen, 7 Feb 1793.

BURNET, GEORGE, of Caskieben, merchant in Aberdeen, 22 Jun and 28 Dec 1764.

BURNET, GEORGE, Capt, of HM 33rd Regiment of Foot, eldest son of **John B** of Elrick, 10 Feb 1777.

BURNET, GEORGE, sometime shipmaster in Peterhead, 4 Aug 1789.

BURNET, JAMES, merchant in Aberdeen, 24 Apr 1788.

BURNET, JAMES, see **William Taylor**.

BURNET, MARY, daughter of late **Robert B** of Sauchen, 9 Dec 1785.

BURNET, ROBERT, merchant in Aberdeen, 20 Dec 1796.

BURNET, ROBERT, Sir, of Leyes, 23 Jan 1768.

BURNS, ROBERT, sometime merchant in Aberdeen, 24 May 1798.

BUTHLAW, WILLIAM, vintner in Aberdeen, 25 Feb 1760.

BUTTER, PATRICK, sometime in Overtoun of Memsie, parish of Rathin, 8 Jun 1787.

BYRES, ROBERT, in Auchleuchries, 4 Mar 1791.

BYRES, WILLIAM, late in Englishtown, parish of Keithhall, 10 Feb 1790.

CADENHEAD, ALEXANDER, shipmaster in Aberdeen, 24 Oct 1794.

CALDER, BARBARA, widow of Mr **Walter Sym**, late minister at Tillinessle, 17 Feb 1775.

CALDER, JOHN, mariner in Aberdeen, 29 Nov 1768.

CAMERON, ANNE, wife of Dr **Donald C**, physician in the parish of St Thomas, Jamaica, 17 Dec 1792.

CAMPBELL, ARCHIBALD, Mr, late minister at Grange. See **Barbara Irvine**, 1795.

CAMPBELL, COLIN, Mr, eldest son of late Mr **Colin C**. minister of Aberdeen, 13 Apr 1765.

CAMPBELL, DONALD, late soldier in the North Fencible regiment, and resident in Aberdeen, 10 Aug 1786.

CAMPBELL, DUNCAN, see **Margaret Campbell.**

CAMPBELL, GEORGE, Dr, principal of the Marischal College of Aberdeen, 3 Mar 1797.

CAMPBELL, MARGARET, Miss, reputed natural daughter of late **Duncan Campbell**, surgeon in the service of the East India Company at Fort Marlborough, on the west coast of Sumatra, 9 Jun 1796.

CAMPBELL, MAY, Miss, resident in Aberdeen, 23 Oct 1788.

CARDNO, ALEXANDER, late in Millhead, 24 Jul 1793.

CARGILL, DAVID, merchant in Aberdeen, 5 Aug 1789.

CASSIE, ANDREW, see **Jean Stewart**:

CATANACH, ALEXANDER, see **Charles Catanach.**

CATANACH, CHARLES, in Bellastraid, in Cromar, and **Alexander C**, his son, 2 Jun 1740 and 13 Jun 1769.

CATANACH, GEORGE, sometime merchant in Aberdeen, 22 Jul 1774.

CATANACH, JAMES, Dr, advocate in Aberdeen, 31 Dec 1761, 13 Jul and 15 Dec 1762, and 19 May 1790.

CATTANACH, WILLIAM, see **Janet Allan.**

CATTO, JOHN, shoemaker in Ellon, 24 Sept 1773.

CHALMERS, ALEXANDER, late of Faichfield, thereafter at Peterhead, 15 Apr 1778.

CHALMERS, CHRISTIAN, see **John Smith.**

CHALMERS, GEORGE, Dr, physician in Aberdeen. See Mrs **Janet Elphinston**.

CHALMERS, JAMES, lintdresser in Aberdeen. See **Jean Donald.**

CHALMERS, JOHN, Dr, principal of the King's College, Aberdeen, 23 Apr 1800.

CHALMERS, ROBERT, cooper in Aberdeen, 19 Jan 1762.

CHALMERS, WILLIAM, merchant, and late provost of Aberdeen, 28 May 1770.

CHALMERS, WILLIAM, Professor of Medicine, King's College, Aberdeen, 22 Jun 1798.

CHRISTALL, ANDREW, sometime in Graysfoord.   See **Christian Corrie**.

CHRISTALL, GILBERT, sometime in Bonnykettle, thereafter in Old Aberdeen, 20 Jun 1764.

CHRISTIE, ALEXANDER, merchant in Aberdeen, 17 Jun 1747 and 28 Oct 1763.

CHRISTIE, WILLIAM, sometime shipmaster in Fraserburgh.   See **Barbara Clark**.

CHRISTIE, WILLIAM, in Muiryhill, parish of Alva, 24 Aug 1796.

CHRUIE, WILLIAM, wright in Lynemore of Carvieside, in Strathdon, 26 Mar 1778.

CLARIHEW, ALEXANDER, residing in Aberdeen, 25 Jul 1782.

CLARIHEW, JAMES, wright in Aberdeen, 30 Jul 1772.

CLARK, BARBARA, widow of **William Christie**, sometime shipmaster in Fraserburgh, 24 Feb 1778.

CLARK, CHRISTIAN, spouse to **Alexander Robertson**, wheelwright in Peterhead, 12 Dec 1772.

CLARK, DONALD, in Little Inverey, 26 Jan 1775.

CLARK, GEORGE, sometime in Nether Foot of Hill, 6 Oct 1790.

CLARK, ISOBELL, sometime resident in Banff, thereafter in Bredach, 9 Mar 1758.

CLARK, JAMES, in Monelly, 21 Nov 1800.

CLARK, JOHN, junior, advocate in Aberdeen, 2 Jan 1768.

CLARK, JOHN, of Kincardine, advocate in Aberdeen, 24 Jun 1778.

CLARK, WILLIAM, in Kinellar, 13 May 1793.

COCKER, HUGH, in Cairnbanno, 27 Apr 1799.

COCKER, JAMES, in Mill of Ord, 29 May 1795.

COOK, JOHN, barrack-master at Braemar Castle, 18 Oct 1781.

COOPER, ALEXANDER, late in Cannabarse, 21 Jun 1785.

COOPER, CHRISTIAN. See **John Bean**.

COOPER, ISABELL, Mrs, sister of late **George C**, goldsmith in Aberdeen, 21 Dec 1769.

COOPER, JAMES, in Mill of Clatt, 24 Feb 1761.

COPLAND, WILLIAM, sometime custom-house clerk in Aberdeen, 30 Mar 1778.

CORBET, GEORGE, in New Gully, 26 Jun 1766.

CORDONER, CHARLES, Mr, Episcopal Minister in Banff, 26 Jan 1795.

CORDONER, JOHN, in Old Deer. See **Helen Rickert**.

CORMACK, JAMES, sailor in Aberdeen, son of **Robert C**, resident in Aberdeen, 12 Feb 1784.

CORMACK, JOHN, mariner, lately residing in Aberdeen. See **Elizabeth Innes**.

COULL, PATRICK, late merchant in Cullen, 23 Nov 1784.

COURAGE, GEORGE, sometime residing in parish of Belhelvie. See **Margaret Gibson**.

COUTS, GEORGE, flaxdresser in Aberdeen, and **Margaret Rae**, his wife, 25 Feb 1779.

COUTS, ISOBEL, in Kilduthie, 21 Sept 1787.

COUTS, JANET, wife of **Charles Findlay** in Craig, 7 Jul 1781.

COWIE, GEORGE, resident in Aberdeen, 17 Sept 1785.

COWIE, WILLIAM, wright in Aberdeen, 5 Feb 1771.

CRAIG, GORDON, late of Brankstown, parish of Inch, 16 Feb and 19 Dec 1795.

CRAIG, NATHANIEL, factor of Pitsligo. See **Helen Mowat**.

CRAIG, ROBERT, in Westertoun of Achlunies, 1 Aug 1769.

CRAWFORD, CHARLES, son of **Patrick C** writer in Aberdeen, 5 Jul 1768.

CRAWFORD, JAMES, shipmaster in Aberdeen, see Mrs **Elizabeth Keith**.

CRAWFORD, PATRICK, messenger in Aberdeen, 4 Sept 1782.

CRAWSHAW, RICHARD, late in Collionaird, 13 Nov 1781, and 21 Aug 1782.

CRICHTON, ANDREW, late in parish of Fyvie. See **Margaret Oliphant**.

CRICHTON, ANDREW, in Crossgight, 9 May 1800.

CRICHTON, WILLIAM, in Clackriach, parish of Old Deer, 29 Jul 1783.

CRIVES, WILLIAM, late of Silverburn, 21 Jan 1790.

CROMAR, GEORGE, in Dykehead, 10 Aug 1769.

CROMBIE, ALEXANDER, at Berryhill, 19 Apr 1782.

CROBMIE, JEAN, widow of **Archibald Reid** in Graystone, 17 June 1780.

CROMBIE, JOHN, merchant in Aberdeen, 13 Sept 1784.

CRUDEN, ALEXANDER, Mr, sometime rector of the parish of South Farnham, Co Essex, in Virginia, and residing in Aberdeen, 8 Aug 1793.

CRUDEN, JAMES, late shipmaster in Fraserburgh, 30 Jun 1783.

CRUDEN, JAMES, dyer at Waukmill of Pitfour, 23 Nov 1797 and 14 Aug 1800.

CRUDEN, JEAN, late in Roseharty, 29 Aug 1775.

CRUDEN, MAY, residing in Aberdeen, daughter of late **William C** merchant, and one of the baillies of Aberdeen, 26 Jun 1790.

CRUICKSHANK, ALEXANDER, at Old Cruives, 24 Aug 1780.

CRUICKSHANK, ALEXANDER, tenant at Woodside, 25 Feb 1783.

CRUICKSHANK, JANET, see **Alexander Strachan**.

CRUICKSHANK, THOMAS, see **Elizabeth Thain**.

CRUICKSHANK, WILLIAM, merchant in Aberdeen, 20 Aug 1779 and 6 Dec 1782.

CULLEN, THOMAS, in Auchnamoon, 3 Oct 1740.

CUMING, ..., in Cullen. See **Margaret Gordon**.

CUMING, ALEXANDER, eldest son of late **James C** merchant in Aberdeen, 26 Jul 1762.

CUMING, ALEXANDER, merchant in Greenbrae, parish of Cruden, 16 Mar 1782.

CUMING, CHARLES, in Tarland, 1 Mar 1799.

CUMING, ELIZABETH, daughter of late **George C** of Pittuly, 30 Dec 1800.

CUMING, JEAN, see **Alexander Loggan**.

CUMING, JOHN, merchant in Aberdeen, 13 Aug 1743, 15 Jan 1756, and 28 Sept 1769.

CUMING, WILLIAM, Mr, minister at Mill of Turriff, 18 Jun 1771. See also **Elizabeth Innes**.

CUMING, WILLIAM, Mr, minister at Rathen, 21 Oct 1800.

CUSHNIE, ISABELLA, sometime residing at Mill of Collairlie, parish of Echt, 28 Jan 1791.

CUSHNIE, ISOBEL, wife of **James Milne**, in Woodside, parish of Tough, 5 Aug 1791.

CUSHNIE, PETER, merchant in Aberdeen, 19 Apr 1799.

CUSHNIE, WILLIAM, merchant in Aberdeen, 11 Jan 1791.

CUTHBERTSON, ALEXANDER, merchant in Aberdeen, 11 Jan 1796.

DALGARNO, ALEXANDER, merchant in Peterhead, 22 Jul 1777 and 27 Aug 1793.

DALGARNO, AMELIA, one of the daughters of the late **James D**, Millhill, 24 Jun 1773.

DALGARNO, HENRIETTA, late servant to James Leslie, merchant in Aberdeen, 9 May 1798.

DALGARNO, ISOBEL, daughter of late **James D** of Millhill, 22 Feb 1773.

DALGARNO, JAMES, late of Millhill, 15 Dec 1767.

DALGARNO, THOMAS, in Longside, 19 Jan 1762.

DAUNEY, FRANCIS, factor on the estate of Haughton. See **Margaret Shepherd**.

DAVIDSON, ALEXANDER, hat manufacturer in Aberdeen, 13 Mar 1790.

DAVIDSON, ALEXANDER, see **Jean Allan.**

DAVIDSON, JAMES, Esq, of Midmar, 4 Dec 1777.

DAVIDSON, JAMES, senior, lime merchant in Aberdeen, 24 Jan 1786.

DAVIDSON, JAMES, shipmaster in Aberdeen, 22 Aug 1787.

DAVIDSON, JOHN, gardener, last residing at Broad Place of Daviot, 19 Jun 1780.

DAVIDSON, JOHN, merchant in Aberdeen, 28 Apr 1800.

DAVIDSON, THOMAS, in Whitehousecroft, near Aberdeen.   See **Marjory Robertson.**

DAVIDSON, WILLIAM, maltster in Hardgate, 15 Oct 1793.

DAVID, JOHN, in Newmilne of Birse, 11 Nov 1794.

DAVID, ROBERT, hosier in Aberdeen, 11 May 1797.

DAY, JAMES, sometime sacrist, King's College, Aberdeen.   See **Elspet Mowat.**

DEANS, JAMES, see **Rachel Stephen**.

DENT, JOHN, of Staindrop in County of Durham, cheesemonger.   See **Janet Mowat.**

DEUCHAR, ALEXANDER, of Comrie, sometime writer in Edinburgh, thereafter in Old Deer, 9 Nov 1756 and 29 Oct 1761.

DEY, JAMES, janitor in King's College, Aberdeen, 28 May 1767.

DIACK, ALEXANDER, in Craigsley, 10 Aug 1781.

DICK, ALEXANDER, sometime servant to late Lord Gardenston, last residing in Peterhead, 14 Jul 1796.

DICKIE, ISOBEL, lately residing in Aberdeen, who was wife of the late **George Panton**, sometime in Old Wrangum, 4 May 1774.

DINGWALL, ALEXANDER, merchant in Aberdeen, 14 Sep 1796.

DINGWALL, JOHN, junior, merchant in Aberdeen, 29 Jul 1778 and 3 Sep 1778.

DINGWALL, JOHN, of Rainiestoun, late merchant in Aberdeen, 25 Jun 1793.

DONALD, JANET, widow of **John Roger**, sometime residing in Aberdeen.   See **Catherine Roger.**

DONALD, JEAN, wife to **James Chalmers**, lintdresser in Aberdeen, 10 May 1776.

DONALD, JOHN, merchant, late one of the bailies of Aberdeen, 28 Oct 1788.

DONALDSON, JAMES, Dr, physician in Aberdeen, 12 Jun 1764.

DOUGLAS, JOHN, Esq, of Tilliquhilly, 2 Jun 1791.

DOVERTY, MARGARET, mantua-maker in Newburgh, 10 Jul 1784.

DUCKIESON, JOSEPH, in Backside of Sinnaboth, 6 Mar 1792.

DUFF, ADAM, of Stockit, merchant, and late Provost of Aberdeen, 10 Dec 1795 and 14 Jan 1799.

DUFF, ALEXANDER, of Hatton, 13 Jun 1765.

DUFF, ISOBEL, residing in the Town of Macduff.　　See Mrs **Isobel Ogilvie.**

DUFF, MARY, Mrs, widow of **William Leslie** of Melross, 14 Jul 1778.

DUFF, PATRICK, Mr, minister of Old Aberdeen, 20 Jul 1784.

DUFF, WILLIAM, Mr, late minister at Keig. 25 Aug 1775.

DUFFUS, JAMES, Mr, in Drumgask, 16 Oct 1762.

DUFFUS, JOHN, blacksmith at Gardenstoun, 30 Jul 1767.

DUGUID, ALEXANDER, sometime of Grenada, thereafter residing in Aberdeen, 14 May 1800.

DUGUID, ANN, in Auchtydonald, 7 Jun 1793.

DUGUID, CHARLES, only son of late **Alexander D** late in Kinbrown of Rothie, 20 May 1767.

DUGUID, JEAN, resident in Old Aberdeen, 3 and 5 Mar 1761.

DUGUID, LESLIE PATRICK, of Balquhain, 10 Dec 1778.

DUGUID, MARGARET, widow of **Andrew Henry,** shipmaster in Peterhead, 29 May 1795.

DUN, WILLIAM, dyer at the Waulkmiln of Craigievar, 17 May 1793.

DUNBAR, JAMES, of Kincorth, 2 Nov 1763.

DUNBAR, JAMES, of Kincorth, sometime residing in Aberdeen, 26 Oct 1772.

DUNBAR, JAMES, Mr, minister at Boyndie.　　See also Mrs **Amelia Nicolson.**

DUNBAR, ROBERT, physician in Banff, 28 Jul 1772.

DUNBAR, ROBERT, in Smidieboyn. See also **Mary Hay.**

DUNBAR, ROBERT, second minister of parish of St Machar, 25 Jan 1788.

DUNCAN, ALEXANDER, junior, merchant in Aberdeen.　　See **Janet Reid.**

DUNCAN, GEORGE, see **Margaret Rolland.**

DUNCAN, ISOBELL, widow of **John Still,** sometime farmer in Cotton, 24 May 1760.

DUNCAN, ISOBEL, sometime wife to **Chevalier Tournier,** otherways French, late tobacconist in Aberdeen, afterwards wife to **John Hill,** residing in Green of Aberdeen, 17 Jan 1798.

UNCAN, JOHN, of Mostown, merchant, and sometime Provost of Aberdeen, 7 Nov 1799.

DUNCAN, LAURENCE, in Pitmuckston, 24 Apr 1780.

DUNCAN, WILLIAM, tenant in Upper Boyndlie, 4 Dec 1766.

DUNCAN, WILLIAM, merchant in Peterhead, 23 Jan 1783.

DUNCAN, WILLIAM, sometime mason in New Deer, thereafter residing in Turiff, 15 Mar 1787.

DURNO, GEORGE, Mr, schoolmaster at Fintray, 21 Jan 1761.

DURWARD, WILLIAM, see **Christian Burnet**.

DUTHIE, ALEXANDER, once planter in Jamaica, thereafter residing in Aberdeen, 19 Jun 1769.

DYCE, ALEXANDER, senior, merchant in Aberdeen, 27 Jan 1774.

DYCE, ALEXANDER, merchant in Aberdeen, 3 Apr 1797.

DYCE, KATHERINE, widow of **Alexander Finnie**, late residing in Aberdeen, 4 Dec 1792.

DYCE, ROBERT, late in Balnakettle, 9 Apr 1773.

EDWARD, JOSEPH, late merchant in Kirkstile of Drumblade, 12 Jul 1773.

ELDER, JAMES, merchant in Aberdeen, 5 Sep 1771.

ELLIS, JAMES, miller at Mill of Chapeltoun, 12 Jun 1792.

ELLIS, WILLIAM, residing at Banff, 19 Apr 1794.

ELLISON, WILLIAM, mariner on board the *Millford* man-of-war. See **Christian Anderson**.

ELMSLIE, ELIZABETH, resident in Aberdeen, only daughter of late **George E**, sometime shipmaster in Aberdeen, afterwards master of the Colloden smack, 12 Oct 1773.

ELMSLIE, GEORGE, see **Elizabeth Elmslie**.

ELPHINSTONE, JANET, Mrs, widow of Dr **George Chalmers**, physician in Aberdeen, 16 Feb 1792.

ELRICK, ALEXANDER, sometime in Wester Craigie, in parish of Belhelvie, 5 Mar 1791.

ELRICK, ROBERT, in Dens, parish of Longside, 20 Oct 1775.

ERSKINE, JAMES, vintner in Aberdeen, 25 Feb 1772.

ESSLEMONT, ANDREW, sometime in Newton of Barnyards of Delgaty, 20 Feb 1760.

ESSLEMONT, WILLIAM, baker in Aberdeen, 15 Apr 1786.

FAIRBAIRN, DOROTHY, Mrs, of Hopewell, lately residing in Aberdeen, 24 Nov 1797.

FALCONER, JAMES, purser RN, sometime in Stonehaven, afterwards residing in the Hardgate of Aberdeen, 17 Nov 1791.

FALCONER, JOHN, of Dum, 18 Oct 1788.

FALCONER, WILLIAM, wheelwright, in parish of Old Deer, 11 Dec 1792.

FARQUHAR, ALEXANDER, late in Westoun, thereafter in Gilcomston. See **Mary Shirras**.

FARQUHAR, ALEXANDER, late farmer in Aucheoch, 28 Feb 1792.

FARQUHAR, HELEN, wife of **Andrew Riddell** in Broomhills, 18 Oct 1792.

FARQUHAR, ISOBELL, housekeeper in Infirmary, Aberdeen, 22 Apr 1795.

FARQUHAR, PATRICK, late in Preistwell, parish of Mortlick, 29 Apr 1792.
FARQUHARSON, ALEXANDER, in Burnroot, 15 May 1761 and 24 Jan 1767. See also **Margaret Milne.**
FARQUHARSON, ALEXANDER, of Balfour, 13 Jan 1792.
FARQUHARSON, ANNA, Mrs, resident in Aberdeen, 12 Aug 1762.
FARQUHARSON, ARCHIBALD, of Finzean, 18 Jun 1798.
FARQUHARSON, CHARLES, see **William Farquharson.**
FARQUHARSON, DONALD, sometime in parish of Strathdon, only son of **John F**, sometime in Wester Micras, 4 Jun 1785.
FARQUHARSON, FRANCIS, of Finzean, 14 Apr 1787.
FARQUHARSON, HARRY, in Milne of Whitehouse, 30 Jan 1766.
FARQUHARSON, JOHN, younger of Monaltrie, 26 Jul 1760.
FARQUHARSON, JOHN, Mr, missionary, minister at Braemar, 20 Jun 1783.
FARQUHARSON, MARGARET, sometime in Prescat, late in Garrowmadie, 5 Dec 1781.
FARQUHARSON, MARY, Miss, residing in Fraserburgh, 14 Feb 1792.
FARQUHARSON, MICHAEL, sometime in Little Inverey, thereafter in Easter Delvorar, 25 May 1767.
FARQUHARSON, WILLIAM, in Milnhead of Melgum, **Margaret Stewart**, his wife, afterwards wife of **Alexander Grant**, in Fechlie, and **Charles F**, their son, 4 Oct 1749, and 4 Apr 1766. See also **Margaret Stewart.**
FARQUHARSON, WILLIAM, in Little Mill of Tough, 18 Jan 1763.
FERGUS, GILBERT, see **Elizabeth Taws.**
FERGUSON, JAMES, Mr, of Pitfour, advocate, 18 Aug 1760.
FERGUSON, JOHN, cooper in Aberdeen, 9 Feb 1773.
FERRIER, JOHN, late ship carpenter in Aberdeen, formerly in Banff, 28 Apr 1794.
FETTES, ALEXANDER, late cartwright in Old Aberdeen, 15 May 1789.
FIDDES, MARGARET, in Fordie, 10 Aug 1769.
FINDLATER, JAMES, late Earl of, 13 Nov 1733, 25 Oct 1764 and 3 Jan 1771.
FINDLAY, CHARLES, in Craig. See **Janet Couts.**
FINNIE, ALEXANDER, late vintner in Aberdeen, 22 Apr 1780.
FINNIE, ALEXANDER, late resident in Aberdeen. See **Katharine Dyce.**
FINNIE, KATHERINE, Miss, residing in Aberdeen, 8 Jun 1791.
FINNIE, WILLIAM, wright in Aberdeen. See **Christiana Anderson.**
FLEMING, JOHN, weaver in Aberdeen. See **Ann Boswell.**
FLORENCE, ALEXANDER, feuar in Old Meldrum, 13 Feb 1777.
FORBES, ALEXANDER, of Blackford, 20 Jun 1751, 17 Jul 1753, and 10 May 1760. See also **Helen Gellie.**

FORBES, ALEXANDER, merchant in Aberdeen, 22 Mar 1797.

FORBES, ALEXANDER, in Mill of Fowles, 13 Nov 1800.

FORBES, ARTHUR, Sir, of Craigievar, Bart, 2 Nov 1776.   See also Dame **Christian Ross**.

FORBES, CHARLES, of Shiells, late Sherriff-Substitute of Aberdeenshire, 17 Apr 1764.

FORBES, CHARLES, resident in Aberdeen, 3 Jun 1783.

FORBES, CHARLES, of Auchernack, 12 Jun 1795.

FORBES, CHRISTIAN, wife of **James Walker**, dyer, sometime at Mill of Auchmedan, now at Walkmill of Crimonmogate, 12 Dec 1772.

FORBES, CHRISTIAN, milliner in Aberdeen, sister of **John F**, younger, of Invereman, 26 Feb 1782.

FORBES, ELIZABETH, Mrs, widow of Mr **George Gordon**, Professor of Oriental Languages in King's College, Aberdeen, 21 Dec and 24 Dec 1773.

FORBES, ELIZABETH, Mrs, daughter of late Capt **John F** of Boyndlie, sometime spouse to late Bailie **George Philip**, merchant in Banff, thereafter wife of late **James Mackie**, late of Gask, residing in Peterhead, 29 Aug 1799.

FORBES, FRANCIS, in Keithack, 12 Aug 1763.

FORBES, FRANCIS, writer in Aberdeen, 21 Dec 1769.

FORBES, GEORGE, junior, merchant in Aberdeen, 21 Aug 1767.

FORBES, GEORGE, coppersmith, and one of the magistrates of Aberdeen, 9 May 1793.

FORBES, GEORGE, of Upper Boyndlie, 30 Dec 1794.

FORBES, ISOBELL, resident in Aberdeen, 14 Nov 1775.

FORBES, JAMES, Lord, 20 Apr 1761.

FORBES, JAMES, resident in Hardgate of Aberdeen, and **Christian Jack**, his spouse, 16 Nov 1761.

FORBES, JAMES and JANET, children of late **William F** of Cairngall, 14 Jun 1794.

FORBES, JANET, Miss, daughter of **Thomas F** of Waterton, 3 Jun 1782.

FORBES, JEAN, widow of Mr **James Leslie**, sometime minister at St Fergus, 9 Dec 1754 and 12 Jun 1777.

FORBES, JEAN, eldest daughter of late **Patrick F** of Shivas, 26 Jun 1789.

FORBES, JOHN, wright at Mill of Strichen, 27 Jun 1764.

FORBES, JOHN, Mr, minister at Udny, 11 Aug 1764.

FORBES, JOHN, of Glencarvey, 21 Feb 1769.

FORBES, JOHN, of Pitsligo, 27 Nov 1781.

FORBES, MARY, Mrs, sister of **Thomas F** of Watertoun, 31 Jul 1770.

FORBES, MARY, spouse to **George Leith**, at Mill of Bodichell, 12 Dec 1772.

FORBES, PATRICK, see **Jean Forbes**.

FORBES, THOMAS, of Watertoun, 22 Jun 1772 and 28 Jan 1777.

FORBES, THOMAS, of Ballogie, 7 Apr 1777.

FORBES, WILLIAM, coppersmith in Aberdeen, 29 Jun and 8 Nov 1762.

FORBES, WILLIAM, in Bagramiln, 26 Jan 1775.

FORBES, WILLIAM, in Tillynaught, 27 Nov 1777.

FORBES, WILLIAM, of Ballogie, 17 Apr 1779.

FORBES, WILLIAM, of Cairngall, 11 Oct 1779.   See also Mrs **Isabell Forsyth**.

FORBES, WILLIAM, resident in Ellon, 31 May 1783.

FORBES, WILLIAM, Mr, minister at Airth.   See also Mrs **Elizabeth Garrioch**.

FORDYCE, ANN and LILLIAS, daughters of late **John F** of Gask, 17 Jul 1764.

FOREMAN, WILLIAM, tenant in Strathburn, 9 Apr 1760.

FORREST, ELIZABETH, widow of **Richard Henderson**, sometime merchant in Fraserburgh, 11 Jun 1792.

FORSYTH, ISABELL, Mrs, widow of **William Forbes** of Cairngall, 14 Jun 1794.

FORSYTH, JAMES, Mr, sometime at Bogson of Tillburies, 13 Jul 1770.

FORSYTH, PATRICK, flaxdresser in Aberdeen, 31 Aug 1769.

FORSYTH, PATRICK, late in Mill of Wartle, 17 Aug 1773.

FORSYTH, WILLIAM, Mr, of Harthill, minister at Aboyne, 23 Jun 1795.

FOTHERINGHAM, WILLIAM, formerly in Mill of Fiddes, afterwards residing in Craighall, 4 Oct 1794.

FOWLER, JAMES, chapman in Aberdeen, 7 Jul 1786.

FRASER, ALEXANDER, sometime farmer in Watertoun of Fingask.   See **Marjory Halket**.

FRASER, ALEXANDER, Mr, minister at Fraserburgh, 16 Jun 1781.

FRASER, ALEXANDER, in Craig of Udny, 11 Mar 1786.

FRASER, ALEXANDER, Hon, of Strichen, one of the Senators of the College of Justice, 2 Feb 1792.

FRASER, ALEXANDER, shipmaster in Peterhead, 25 Apr 1796.

FRASER, FRANCIS, elder of Findrack, 21 Nov 1792.

FRASER, ISAAC, vintner in Aberdeen, 2 Aug 1800.

FRASER, JAMES, in Buchaam, 16 Jun 1781.

FRASER, JAMES, late farmer in Newseat of St Fergus, 13 Jun 1786.

FRASER, JOHN, in Wester Micras, 20 Dec 1791.

FRASER, JOHN, hosier in Aberdeen.   See **Rebecca Gibbon**.

FRASER, THOMAS, in Tolmaads, 31 Jan 1798.

FRASER, WILLIAM, sometime advocate in Aberdeen, thereafter in Peterhead, 15 Jan 1760.

FRENCH, JOHN, advocate in Aberdeen, 28 Jun and 23 Sep 1762, and 2 Jul 1764.

FROST, JOHN, late merchant in Aberdeen, 7 Feb 1783.

FULLEN (FULTON), JAMES, sometime gardener at Ythan Lodge and thereafter residing in Aberdeen, 3 Mar 1785.

FYFE, JOHN, sometime in Invercharrach of Cabrach, 5 Jul 1773.

FYFE, JOHN, formerly surgeon in HM Navy, lately residing in Aberdeen, 18 Jul 1794.

GALL, ALEXANDER, Mr, preacher in Aberdeen, 25 Jul 1771.

GALL, PATRICK, in Foggyrigg, parish of Rain, 7 Sep and 7 Oct 1784. See **Jean Beattie.**

GALL, WILLIAM, merchant in Lumbs, 27 Dec 1787.

GALLOWAY, MARJORY, widow of **John Watt**, in Logie, 4 Jan 1781.

GAMMOCK, WILLIAM, farmer in Coburty, 3 Feb 1785.

GARDEN, ALEXANDER, workman in Aberdeen. See **Janet Simpson**.

GARDEN, ALEXANDER, of Troup, 6 Mar 1786, 12 Mar 1792, and 22 Dec 1794.

GARDEN, ANN, Mrs, widow of **James Innes**, provost, merchant in Banff, 22 Feb 1772.

GARDEN, JAMES, merchant in Aberdeen. See **Mrs Jean Yeats**.

GARDEN, JOHN, late at Gateside of Newpark, in the parish of Newhills, 3 Apr 1797.

GARDNER, GEORGE, sometime in Blairshinnoch. See **Elizabeth Morison.**

GARE (GAIR), HUGH, travelling chapman in Huntly, 10 Jul 1770.

GARRIOCH, ALEXANDER, late minister at Midmar. See **Mrs Isobell Gordon.**

GARROCH, ANDREW, merchant in Aberdeen, 2 Oct 1770.

GARRIOCH, ELIZABETH, Mrs, residing in Aberdeen, widow of Mr **William Forbes**, minister at Airth, 15 Jul 1790.

GARRIOCH, ROBERT, see **Bess McGowan.**

GEDDES, JAMES, merchant in Gardenston, 7 Jul 1787.

GELLAN, ANDREW, son of late **Alexander G**, butcher in Aberdeen, 15 May 1760.

GELLAN, JOHN, Capt of 66th Regiment of Foot, 20 May 1783.

GELLIE, HELEN, see **Alexander Forbes.**

GEMBELL, JOHN, late vintner in Aberdeen, 16 Dec 1779.

GEORGE, JAMES, feuar in Turriff, 3 Nov 1783.

GEORGE, WILLIAM, tenant in Cortiecram, and **Janet Annand**, his widow, 15 Jun 1762.

GERARD, ALEXANDER, Dr, Professor of Divinity in King's College, Aberdeen, 15 Jun 1795.

GERARD, CHRISTIAN, see **William Gerard**.

GERARD, GEORGE, late in Finnagad, parish of Ordiequie, 15 Nov 1773.

GERARD, GEORGE, junior, of Midstrath, residing at Haughs of Ashogle, 12 Jan 1799.

GERARD, GILBERT, advocate in Aberdeen, 23 Jun 1767 and 10 Dec 1781.

GERARD, WILLIAM, in Corsefold, and **Christian G**, his daughter, 30 Nov 1773.

GIBBON, REBECCA, widow of **John Fraser**, hosier in Aberdeen, 7 Mar 1792.

GIBSON, ANDREW, tenant in Fiddesbegg, 8 Mar 1774.

GIBSON, JAMES, late in Seafield, eldest son of **James G**, in Upper Brogar, 30 Nov 1791.

GIBSON, MARGARET, widow of **George Courage**, sometime residing in parish of Belhelvie, and daughter of late **James G**, sometime residing in Upper Broggan, parish of Slains, 14 Feb 1791.

GILCHRIST, ALEXANDER, late dyer in Old Rain,, 2 Jul 1785.

GILCHRIST, HARRY, late Lieutenant in 42nd Regiment of Foot, 18 Jan 1780.

GILCHRIST, MARGARET, Mrs, lately residing in Peterhead, widow of Lt **Harry G**, late 42nd Regiment of Foot, 24 May 1796.

GILL, ALEXANDER, resident in Banff, 21 Feb 1769.

GILL, DAVID, shoemaker in Bowbridge of Aberdeen, 27 Jan 1795.

GILL, DAVID, see **Margaret Shepherd**.

GILL, GEORGE, shipmaster in Fraserburgh, 8 Feb 1762.

GILLENDERS, BARBARA, widow of **Alexander Webster**, sometime in Tarland, 3 Mar 1797.

GILLESPIE, JOHN, late gardener at Kittybrewster, 6 Apr 1798.

GLASS, DONALD, sometime in Etnach, thereafter in Bellamore, 5 May 1767.

GLENNY, ARTHUR, wright at Causeway. See **Marjory Tholson**.

GLENNY, JOHN, see **William Snawie**.

GODSMAN, JOHN, late in Upper Achwadly, 10 Aug 1781.

GOODBRAND, GEORGE, son of late **Alexander G**, sometime in Portsoy, 29 Aug (16 Sep) 1760.

GORDON, ... of Hopshill. See Mrs **Margaret Milne**.

GORDON, ALEXANDER, of Edintore, 16 Mar 1763.

GORDON, ALEXANDER, of Coldwalls, and **Patrick G**, his son, 28 Jul 1763.

GORDON, ALEXANDER, merchant in Boulogne-sur-la-mer, France. See **Mary Shirras**.

GORDON, ALEXANDER, of Gight, 18 Dec 1778.

GORDON, ALEXANDER, Esq of Letterourie, 17 Apr 1797.

GORDON, ALEXANDER, late in Redmire, 18 Jul 1800.

GORDON, ANNE, widow of Mr **John Barclay**, Episcopal Minister at Peterhead, 28 Feb 1766.

GORDON, ARTHUR, of Wardhouse, 24 Sep 1761.

GORDON, CHARLES, in Belnakyle, 24 Jan 1771.

GORDON, CHARLES, of Fetter Angus. See **Margaret Stewart**.

GORDON, CHARLES, of Auchleuchries, 15 Sep 1777.

GORDON, CHARLES, of Abergeldie, 17 May 1796 and 16 Nov 1797.

GORDON, CHARLES, of Blelack. See Mrs **Anne Urquhart**.

GORDON, ELIZABETH, widow of **Arthur G** of Wardhouse, 31 Jul 1764.

GORDON, ELIZABETH, Mrs, only child of the late **John G**, shipmaster in Aberdeen, wife of Mr **George Mark**, minister at Peterculter, 22 Dec 1797.

GORDON, ELIZABETH, Miss, daughter of the late **Charles G** of Buthlaw, 27 Apr 1797.

GORDON, FRANCES, Miss, daughter of late **John G** of Baldornie, 4 Aug 1792.

GORDON, GEORGE, of Shilagreen, 15 Jun 1778.

GORDON, GEORGE, Mr, minister of Drumblade, 7 Jun 1764.

GORDON, GEORGE, Mr, Professor of Oriental Languages in King's College, Aberdeen. See Mrs **Elizabeth Forbes**.

GORDON, GEORGE, of Gight, 9 Oct 1779. See also Mrs **Katharine Innes**.

GORDON, GEORGE, merchant in Aberdeen, 14 Apr 1784.

GORDON, HELEN, sometime wife to **James Innes**, and thereafter widow of **James Alexander**, wright in Banff, 11 Oct 1798.

GORDON, HUGH, only son of the late **George G**, of Cults, 29 Jul 1762.

GORDON, ISABELL, Mrs, of Edintore, widow of **Alexander Garrioch**, late minister at Midmar, 24 Dec 1778.

GORDON, ISABELL, Miss, daughter of **Alexander G**, of Logie, 20 Jul 1780.

GORDON, JAMES, late in Laggan of Auchindoun, 4 Apr 1764 and 12 May 1774.

GORDON, JAMES, late in Auchleuchries, residing in Aberdeen, 17 Sep (Aug) 1776.

GORDON, JAMES, of Badenscoth, 21 Dec 1778.

GORDON, JAMES, Esq, late of Letterfowrie, 4 Oct 1790 and 17 Dec 1791.

GORDON, JOHN, late in Craibstoun, 9 Mar 1762.

GORDON, JOHN, in Balmoral, 4 Feb 1767.

GORDON, JOHN, of Crathienaird, 28 Feb 1767 and 3 Mar 1769.

GORDON, JOHN, of Birkenbush, 20 Jun 1782.

GORDON, JOHN, of Allanaquoich, 19 Mar 1784.

GORDON, JOHN, sometime of Crichie, second son of late **John G,** of Kinnellar, 25 Feb 1788.

GORDON, JOHN, late in Whitehouse of Maryculter, 13 Jul 1792.

GORDON, JOHN, Dr, sometime minister of St Paul's Chapel, Aberdeen. See Mrs **Ann Burnet.**

GORDON, JOHN, late salmon-fisher at Bridge of Don, 15 Mar 1793.

GORDON, JOHN, junior, advocate in Aberdeen, 9 Oct 1793.

GORDON, KATHARINE, Mrs, daughter of **George G**, of Carnousie, lately residing in Banff, 1 Aug 1764.

GORDON, KATHERINE, Lady, daughter of **Cosmo George**, Duke of Gordon, and wife of Capt **Thomas Booker**, late of 53rd Regiment, 13 Jun 1797.

GORDON, LUDOVICK, in Tomnagailach, 1 Sep 1786.

GORDON, MARGARET, Miss, youngest daughter of late **George G,** of Gight, 22 Feb 1783.

GORDON, MARGARET, Miss, daughter of late Mr **Thomas G**, Professor of Philosophy in the King's College of Aberdeen, 1 Aug 1797.

GORDON, MARY, Mrs, residing in Banff, widow of **Thomas Innes** of Muiryfold, 17 Feb 1784.

GORDON, MARY, Mrs, widow of **Alexander G,** officer of Excise in Old Meldrum, 13 Jul 1791.

GORDON, MARY, Mrs, lately residing in Banff, daughter of **Charles G**, of Buthlaw, 6 and 7 Jul 1795.

GORDON, PATRICK, Excise officer in Portsoy, 7 Apr 1794.

GORDON, PATRICK, see **Alexander Gordon.**

GORDON, PETER, of Mosstown, 4 Mar 1795.

GORDON, RICHARD, Mr, of Craigmyle, advocate in Aberdeen, 22 Dec 1763 and 20 Dec 1765.

GORDON, ROBERT, of the Navy, residing at Aberdeen. See Mrs **Jane Grant.**

GORDON, ROBERT, tenant in Raemoir, 26 Dec 1777.

GORDON, THOMAS, Mr, see Mrs **Elizabeth Innes.**

GORDON, THOMAS, Mr, in Achtochrach of Glenrinnes, 8 Jan 1795.

GORDON, WILLIAM, Admiral of the British Navy, lately residing in Banff, 27 Aug 1774.

GORDON, WILLIAM, of Nethermuir, 7 Feb 1775.

GORDON, WILLIAM, of Shilagreen, 13 Jan 1777.

GORDON, WILLIAM, at Haughs of Ashogle, 19 Apr 1781.

GORDON, of Hopshill. See Mrs **Margaret Milne**.

GRANT, ALEXANDER, see **William Farquharson**.

GRANT, ANNE, wife of **Patrick Mackie**, wright at Causeway, 3 Jul 1781.

GRANT, ARCHIBALD, Sir, of Monymusk, Bart, 17 Jun 1779 and 24 Feb 1797.

GRANT, GEORGE, Mr, late minister at Rathven, 5 Jun 1789 and 15 Feb 1790.

GRANT, HELEN, widow of **John G,** in Alachallagan, 23 Dec 1776.

GRANT, alias MILLAR, JAMES, in Little Tullich, and **Isabell Stewart**, his wife, 5 Nov 1756 and 20 Oct 1761.

GRANT, JANE, Mrs, late wife of Lt **Robert Gordon** of the Navy, residing at Aberdeen, 30 Dec 1774.

GRANT, JOHN, of Rothmaise, 5 Jan 1767, 28 Mar 1771, 25 Jul 1772, 29 Oct 1788 and 5 Aug 1791.

GRANT, JOHN, late in Tombreck, parish of Strathdon, 22 Sep 1780.

GRANT, PETER LESLIE, of Balquhain, Esq, 17 Nov 1774.

GRANT, SAMUEL, leather merchant in Aberdeen, 13 Jul 1790.

GRANT, WILLIAM, late sergeant in 53rd Regiment of Foot, 23 Dec 1777.

GRASSICH, JAMES, son of **James G**, in Pantiland, 12 Mar 1789.

GRAY, ALEXANDER, in Oldwhat, 2 Sep 1760.

GRAY, ALEXANDER, sometime on Stonyhill of Cruden, 2 Dec 1762.

GRAY, ANDREW, merchant in Aberdeen. See Mrs **Jean Yeats**.

GRAY, CHRISTIAN, widow of **David Low**, shipmaster in Aberdeen, 9 Dec 1789.

GRAY, GEORGE, in Craufoord, and **Jean Alexander**, his spouse, 13 Feb 1760.

GRAY, GEORGE, late in Hopishill, 18 Jan 1764.

GRAY, JAMES, residing in Aberdeen, 29 Nov 1785.

GRAY, JOHN, late in Gateside of Pitullie, 3 Aug 1790.

GRAY, ROBERT, merchant in Ellon, 18 Jul 1794.

GRAY, WILLIAM, sometime in Cultercullen. See **Alexander Ironside**.

GREGORY, JOHN, son of late **Gregor G**, in Torran, 5 Mar 1771.

GREIG, JAMES, at Waulkmill of Hythie, 11 Mar 1783.

GRIERSON, JAMES, see **James McGregor**.

GRIACH, JAMES, in Coutlach, 15 Feb 1787. See also **Margaret Thomson**.

GRIGG, JOHN, in Ardfour, 29 Oct 1783.

GUTHRIE, ALEXANDER, Sir, of Ludquharn, 19 Jan 1762.

GUTHRIE, ANDREW, Mr, minister at Peterhead, 22 Feb 1782.

HALKET, MARJORIE, widow of **Alexander Fraser**, sometime farmer in Watertoun of Fingask, 23 Nov 1773.

HALKET, WILLIAM, Mr, schoolmaster in Turriff, 17 Apr 1768.

HAMILTON, JOHN, sometime wharffinger at London, lately residing in Portsoy, 16 Jan 1783.

HARDIE, JAMES, sometime merchant, afterwards shoemaker in Old Meldrum, 24 Jun 1791.

HARPER, FRANCIS, in Balnaboth, parish of Birse, 2 Aug 1791.

HARROW, ELSPET, sometime wife to **George H**, stabler in Aberdeen, thereafter wife to **James Innes**, residing in the Gallowgate of Aberdeen, 28 Nov 1791.

HARROWAY, GEORGE, shipmaster in Banff, 4 Oct 1774.

HARVIE, ALEXANDER, sometime maltster in Aberdeen, 6 Sep 1780.

HAY, ANDREW, of Rannas, 18 Mar 1791.

HAY, ANNA, see Mr **Hugh Hay**.

HAY, ELIZABETH, widow of **William Beet**, blacksmith in Aberdeen, 14 Apr 1791.

HAY, GEORGE, in Denhead of Gask, 29 Jun 1793.

HAY, HUGH, Mr, one of the ministers of Aberdeen, and Miss **Anna H**, his sister, children of late Dr **James H**, 3 Jun 1793.

HAY, JAMES, dyer at Bridgend of Fyvie. See **Margaret Pratt**.

HAY, JOHN, in Delgaty, 23 Dec 1760.

HAY, JOHN, Esq, of Mount Blairy, 19 Nov 1785.

HAY, MARGARET, in Burnside of Tynet, 31 Jul 1783.

HAY, MARY, sometime in Craibstoun, widow of **Robert Dunbar**, sometime in Smithyboyn, 12 Dec 1757 and 30 Jun 1785.

HEATON, JOHN, farmer in Oldwhat, 29 May 1794.

HECTOR, ISABELL, in Hardgate of Aberdeen, wife of **James Aiken**, soldier in Colonel Gordon's Regiment of Foot, 26 Jan 1779.

HECTOR, JAMES, mason in Aberdeen. See **Jean Volum**.

HEDDERWICK, GEORGE, gardener in Aberdeen, 14 Jun 1763.

HENDERSON, ALEXANDER, wright in Aberdeen, 20 Feb 1784.

HENDERSON, DAVID, late merchant in Newbyth, 4 Apr 1777 and 16 Apr 1778.

HENDERSON, RICHARD, sometime merchant in Fraserburgh.   See **Elizabeth Forrest**.

HENDERSON, WILLIAM, sometime writer in Edinburgh, thereafter residing at Newseat of St Fergus, 23 Sep and 30 Nov 1761.

HENDERSON, WILLIAM, merchant in Fraserburgh, 11 Jun 1792.

HENDRY, ANDREW, sometime shipmaster in Peterhead, 1 Jun 1796.
   See also **Margaret Duguid**.

HENDRY, GEORGE, late in Old Maad, 13 Jan 1795.

HENDRY (HENRY),JANET, see **George Alexander**.

HENDRY, JEAN, in Mormond, village of Strichen, 5 Aug 1795.

HEPBURN, ALEXANDER, sometime ground officer at Techmuiry, parish of Fraserburgh, 12 Dec 1785.

HERDMAN, THOMAS, Capt, shipmaster in Aberdeen, 2 May 1769.

HERRIEGERRIE, GEORGE, in Colpy, parish of Culsalmond. See **Janet Mennie**.

HILL, ALEXANDER, merchant in Kintore, 19 Jun 1779.

HILL, JOHN, residing in Green of Aberdeen, 17 Jan 1798. See also **Isabel Duncan**.

HOG, ANN, residing in Hardgae of Aberdeen, widow of **James Scott**, sometime farmer in Baghadlie, 11 Dec 1799.

HOPE, JOHN, resident in Aberdeen. See **Ann Paul**.

HORN, JAMES, in Old Westhall, 2 Oct 1764.

HORN, JOHN, at Well of Spa, near Aberdeen, 31 Aug 1780.

HOWIE, ALEXANDER, Mr, minister at Tarves, 19 Jun 1767.

HUDART, CATHERINE, Mrs, residing in Aberdeen, widow of **Andrew Lunan**, glazier there, 21 Jan 1796.

HUME, CHARLES, in Netherton of Lethenty, parish of Daviot, 11 Aug 1797.

HUME, JOHN, shipmaster in Aberdeen, 14 Mar 1798.

HUNTER, ALEXANDER, in Gourdis, 4 Aug 1785.

HUNTER, JOHN, in Mill of Blairdens, 11 Sep 1795.

HUNTER, JOHN, merchant in Meikle Gourdas, 7 Feb 1799.

HUNTER, WILLIAM, in Broomhillock, 13 Oct 1800.

HUTCHEON, GEORGE, merchant in Old Aberdeen, 7 Aug 1770 and 2 Aug 1774.

HUTCHEON, JAMES, merchant in Tarland, 2 Nov 1795.

HUTCHEON, ROBERT, at Outscats, parish of Old Machar, 23 Sep 1785.

HUTCHESON, PETER, merchant in Peterhead, 11 Jun 1795.

HUTCHESON, ROBERT, flaxdresser in Aberdeen, 29 Jan 1788.

IMRIE, ALEXANDER, manufacturer in Aberdeen, 14 Aug 1800.

IMRIE, JOHN, schoolmaster in Lumphanan, 7 Nov 1768.

INGRAM, CHARLES, stabler in Aberdeen, 15 Jul 1774.

INGRAM, DONALD, late in Easter Mains of Auchinhove, 3 Apr 1779.

INGRAM, JOHN, merchant in Old Meldrum, 17 Jul 1764.

INNES, ALEXANDER, commissary clerk of Aberdeen, 23 Oct 1790.

INNES, ALEXANDER, and ARTHUR SINCLAIR I, children of **William I**, late merchant in Thurso, presently residing in Aberdeen, 8 Feb 1793.

INNES, ALEXANDER, of Breda, 31 Dec 1798.

INNES, ARTHUR SINCLAIR, see **Alexander Innes**.

INNES, ELIZABETH, widow of Mr **William Cumming**, minister at Mill of Turriff, 15 Jan 1791.

INNES, ELIZABETH, widow of **John Cormack**, mariner, lately residing in Aberdeen, 11 Jun 1793.

INNES, ELIZABETH, Mrs, widow of Mr **Thomas Gordon**, Professor of Philosophy in King's College, Aberdeen, 22 Aug 1799.

INNES, ELSPETH, see **George Riddoch**.

INNES, HUGH, Mr, sometime minister at Mortlack. See **Elizabeth Abernethy**.

INNES, JAMES, see Mrs **Ann Garden**.

INNES, JAMES, see **Elspet Harrow**.

INNES, JAMES, see **Helen Gordon**.

INNES, JOHN, of Muiryfold, residing in Banff, 7 Mar 1781.

INNES, JOHN, in Netherton of Wester Auchmore, 21 Dec 1789.

INNES, JOSEPH, of Pitmedden, 14 Mar 1800.

INNES, KATHARINE, Mrs, widow of **George Gordon**, of Gight, 22 Feb 1783.

INNES, PETER, Capt, lately residing in Aberdeen, 12 Feb 1789.

INNES, ROBERT, town-clerk of Banff, 4 Jul 1783.

INNES, THOMAS, of Muiryfold. See Mrs **Mary Gordon**.

IRONSIDE, ALEXANDER, in Fiddesbeg, and **William Gray**, sometime in Cultercullen, 28 Aug 1777.

IRONSIDE, JOHN, in Backhill, 10 Dec 1764.

IRONSIDE, JOHN, sometime in Auchreddy, parish of New Deer, 9 Aug 1785 and 29 Dec 1786.

IRONSIDE, WILLIAM, in Muirden, parish of Alva, 25 Jul 1782.

IRVINE, ANN, Mrs, widow of **Colin Allan**, late goldsmith in Aberdeen, 14 Feb 1799.

IRVINE, BARBARA, residing in Aberdeen, widow of Mr **Archibald Campbell**, late minister at Grange, 20 Oct 1795.

IRVINE, CHARLES, Mr, late merchant in Gottenburg, thereafter residing in Aberdeen, 22 Nov 1771.

IRVINE, CHARLES, Dr, sometime of St Thomas, Jamaica, but late of Aberdeen, 11 Jun 1794.

IRVINE, ELIZABETH, Mrs, duaghter of late **Robert I** at Kinmundy, 22 Apr 1788.

IRVINE, GEORGE, of Boyndlie, 21 Apr 1798.

IRVINE, HELEN, widow of **Alexander Walker**, late provost of Aberdeen, 15 Jul 1756.

IRVINE, HELEN, daughter of late **Arthur I,** factor of Drum, 15 Dec 1769.

IRVINE, JOHN, Mr, formerly of Gothenburg, thereafter residing in Aberdeen, 23 Mar 1795.

IRVINE, JOHN, tanner at Well of Spa, near Aberdeen, 31 May 1798.

JACK, CHRISTIAN, see **James Forbes.**

JAFFRAY, ALEXANDER, late in Old Meldrum, 8 Dec 1798.

JAFFRAY, MARY, late in Corthies, 19 Dec 1791.

JAFFRAY, ROBERT, merchant and farmer in Carniehill, 23 Mar 1769.

JAMIESON (JAMESON), ALEXANDER, in Skellybogs, 9 Jul 1772.

JAMIESON, ALEXANDER, late in Whitecairns of Belhelvie, 30 Nov 1789.

JAMIESON, ALEXANDER, in Little Gight, parish of Fyvie, 16 Dec 1789.

JAMIESON, ALEXANDER, clerk to Messrs Hugh Gordon and Co, merchants in Aberdeen, 14 Oct 1797.

JAMIESON, CHARLES, Esq, sometime of the parish of St George, Hanover Square, Co Middlesex, gentleman, afterwards residing in Aberdeen, 27 Sep 1791.

JAMIESON, GEORGE, merchant in Skellybogs, 9 Jul 1772.

JAMIESON, GEORGE, gardener in Aberdeen, 20 Dec 1796.

JAMIESON, JAMES, in Pouckburn, 23 Dec 1777.

JAMIESON, JAMES, in Cairncummar, 5 Jul 1799.

JAMIESON, JANET, wife of **John Kirktown**, late woolcomber in Spittal, and presently soldier in the Aberdeenshire Regiment, 18 Nov 1795.

JAMIESON, JOHN, tailor in Whitefield, 1 Sep 1761.

JAMIESON, JOHN, in Upper Kebbaty, parish of Midmar, 6 Aug 1799.

JESSAMIN, ANN, wife of **John Menzies**, merchant in Aberdeen, 28 Feb 1770.

JOHNSTON, ALEXANDER, maltster in Aberdeen, 4 Aug 1761.

JOHNSTON, ALEXANDER, in Burnside of Schivas, 17 Nov 1767.

JOHNSTON, ALEXANDER, merchant in Peterhead, 29 Aug 1769.

JOHNSTON, ALEXANDER, Mr, minister at Alford, 2 Jun 1778.

JOHNSTON, DAVID, Mr, sometime schoolmaster at Chapel of Garioch, 12 Jul 1787.

JOHNSTON, ELSPET, resident in Aberdeen, 20 Jun 1775.

JOHNSTON, JAMES, Rev Mr, minister at Crimond, 21 Jun 1796.

JOHNSTON, JAMES, sometime in Mains of Ardo, thereafter residing in Old Aberdeen, 29 Jan 1800.

JOHNSTON, JAMES, farmer in Oldtown of Ardendraught, 18 Jul 1800.

JOHNSTON, JOSEPH, sometime quartermaster in 10th Regiment of Foot. See **Jane Paterson**.

JOHNSTON, KATHARINE, Mrs, residing at Lochhead, widow of **James J**, late bleacher there, 2 Jul 1800.

JOHNSTON, WILLIAM, of Badifurrow, 23 Jul 1764.

JOPP, JAMES, of Cotton, merchant, and late provost of Aberdeen, 21 Oct 1794.

JOPP, JOHN, in Kirktoun of Drumblade. See **Helen Leslie**.

JOSS, JOHN, of Colloinart. See Mrs **Mary Ogilvie**.

JOYNER, ALEXANDER, tailor in Aberdeen, 13 Jun 1798.

KEILLO, JEAN, widow of **John Robson**, sometime in Lasts, 18 Jul 1763.

KEIR, GREGOR, in Little Inverey, 16 Feb 1768.

KEITH, ANNE, daughter of late **James K**, of Bruxie, 21 Sep 1762.

KEITH, ANNE, sometime residing in Aberdeen, 2 Mar 1792.

KEITH, ELIZABETH, Mrs, residing in Aberdeen, widow of **James Crawford,** shipmaster in Aberdeen, 27 Jul 1773 and 5 Oct 1775.

KEITH, ROBERT, gardener in Aberdeen, 29 Sep 1778.

KEITH, WILLIAM, sometime in Mill of Artannes, thereafter in Beins, 11 Nov 1761.

KELLAS, JANET, in Letterfury, 1 Oct 1766.

KEMP, ALEXANDER, shoemaker in Spittal, near Aberdeen, 7 Feb 1775.

KENNEDY, ALEXANDER, shipmaster in Fraserburgh, 9 Aug 1771.

KENNEDY, WILLIAM, Mr, Professor of Greek in Marishall College of Aberdeen, 31 Jan 1786.

KIDD, JOHN, in Rora. See **Grizel Scott**.

KILGOUR, PATRICK, dyer in Nether Kinmundy, 5 Oct 1774.

KING, KATHERINE, spouse to late **Thomas Lumsden**, goldsmith and jeweller in Aberdeen, 18 Feb 1773.

KINTORE, JOHN, Earl of, 17 Oct 1723 and 31 Oct 1769.

KIRKTOWN, JOHN, late woolcomber in Spittal, and presently soldier in the Aberdeenshire Regiment. See **Janet Jamieson**.

KNOWLES, ALEXANDER, shipmaster in Aberdeen, 19 May 1780.

KNOWLES, GEORGE, Mr, late minister of Birse, 13 Nov 1789.

KNOX, JAMES, late vintner at Newburgh, 2 Dec 1800.

KYNOCH, JAMES, merchant in Aberdeen, 20 May 1783.

KYNOCH, WILLIAM, mealseller in Aberdeen, 5 Sep 1782 and 1 Apr 1783.

LAIRD, JAMES, in Muir of Alfoord, 29 Jan 1763.

LAMB, JAMES, tailor in Aberdeen, 6 Feb 1783.

LAMOND, JAMES, in Newbigging of Glencluny, 2 May 1769.

LARGOE (LARGUE), GEORGE, in Sockoch, 20 Dec 1763.

LARGOE, GEORGE, Mr, minister at Rathen, 1 Oct 1771.

LARGOE, MARGARET, in Fraserburgh, widow of **William Watson**, late farmer in Whitehall, parish of Tyrie, 3 Dec 1789.

LAUDER, JANET, Mrs, daughter of Sir **Robert L**, of Balmouth, 3 Nov 1780.

LAURENCE, ALEXANDER, in Newknock, 4 Jun 1783.

LAURENCE, ISABEL, residing in Aberdeen, 5 Jul 1798.

LAURIE, WILLIAM, weaver in Aberdeen, 7 Dec 1793.

LAWSON, GEORGE, carpenter at Footdee, 12 Jun 1788.

LAWSON, JAMES, merchant in Banff, 2 Feb 1749, 21 Mar 1751, 17 Mar 1756 and 19 Sep 1760.

LEGG, GILBERT, farmer at Mill of Tillienamoult, thereafter at Ellon, 14 Mar 1765.

LEITH, ALEXANDER, Mr, one of the masters of the Grammar School of Aberdeen, 19 Apr 1799.

LEITH, GEORGE, in Delrossa, 1 May 1760.

LEITH, GEORGE, of Blackhall, 26 Apr 1771.

LEITH, JOHN, of Blair, 23 Oct 1765.

LEITH, LAURENCE, sometime resident in Aberdeen, 25 Feb 1779.

LENDRUM, PETER, burgess of Old Aberdeen, 19 Jun 1771.

LEONARD, JOHN, Chelsea pensioner in Aberdeen, 19 Feb 1765.

LESLIE (LESLY), ALEXANDER, of Warthill, 2 Jun 1724 and 7 Aug 1766.

LESLIE, ALEXANDER, of Berryden, merchant in Aberdeen, 19 May 1800.

LESLIE, GEORGE, merchant in Aberdeen, 28 Jul 1789.

LESLIE, GEORGE, resident in Bithnie, parish of Forbes, 12 Jan 1791.

LESLIE, GEORGE, late in Borrowstoun, parish of Newhills, thereafter residing in Aberdeen, 31 May 1791.

LESLIE, GEORGE, surgeon in Tochar, 30 Jun 1791.

LESLIE, GEORGE, Esq, late if Jamaica, afterwards residing in Old Aberdeen, 24 May 1796.

LESLIE, HELEN, lately residing in Old Meldrum, widow of **James Webster**, sometime blacksmith in Inverury, 10 Aug 1784.

LESLIE, HELEN, wife of **John Jopp**, in Kirktoun of Drumblade, 20 Dec 1786.

LESLIE, JAMES, see **Jean Forbes**.

LESLIE, JEAN, daughter of **John L** of Drumdollo, and late spouse to Mr **George Abercrombie**, minister in Aberdeen, 5 Aug 1777.

LESLIE, JOHN, merchant in Aberdeen, 16 May 1776 and 17 Jun 1777.

LESLIE, JOHN, late in Cottburn, parish of Turriff, 18 May 1792.

LESLIE, MARGARET, sometime in Clola, second daughter of late **George L**, of Coburtie, 23 Jul 1776.

LESLIE, ROBERT, late at Millton of Collarlie, 13 Jun 1775.

LESLIE, ROBERT, late merchant at Monymusk, 6 May 1799.

LESLIE, WILLIAM, of Melross, 4 Dec 1776. See also Mrs **Mary Duff**.

LESLIE, WILLIAM, sometime factor of Muchals, thereafter residing in Aberdeen, 5 May 1777.

LICKLY, WILLIAM, cartwright at the Gallowgate head of Aberdeen, 31 Dec 1790.

LIDDERDALE, MARY, daughter of late **James L**, of Forres, 22 Jul 1786.

LILLIE, WILLIAM, late in Kirkton of St Fergus, 21 Nov 1792.

LIND, ADAM, merchant in Tarves, 6 Feb and 31 Dec 1760 (31 Jul 1764).

LIND, ISOBEL, resident in Aberdeen, 4 Aug 1785.

LINDSAY, THOMAS, in Knock, 20 Jul 1768.

LITTLEJOHN, JAMES, in Haughs of Edinglassie, 16 Dec 1788.

LIVINGSTON, CHRISTIAN, late mariner on board the *Mary*, lying in the harbour of Aberdeen, 17 Jan 1798.

LIVINGSTON, THOMAS, Dr, physician in Aberdeen, 12 Aug 1785.

LOBBAN, GEORGE, sometime landwaiter in Aberdeen. See **Anne Rose**.

LOGAN, ALEXANDER, sometime in Uppertoun of Straloch, afterwards in White Rashes, parish of New Machar, and **Jean Cummine**, his wife, 27 Jan 1789.

LONGMORE, JOHN, late in Milltown of Deskford, 21 Oct 1800.

LORIMER, JOHN, merchant in Portsoy, 20 Nov 1770 and 8 Dec 1772.

LORIMER, PATRICK, sometime resident in Portsoy, 15 Feb 1771.

LOW, ALEXANDER, in Wester Cairney, 11 Dec 1769.

LOW, GEORGE, blacksmith in Aberdeen, and **Isobel Orcherton**, his wife, 18 Nov 1790.

LOW, HERCULES, sometime surgeon in Aberdeen, 9 Feb 1776.

LOW, JOHN, farmer in Cairnorie, 10 Sep 1799.

LUMSDEN, ALEXANDER, advocate in Aberdeen, 6 May 1777 and 28 Sep 1778.

LUMSDEN, ALEXANDER, Dr, physician in Aberdeen, 21 Mar 1778.

LUMSDEN, DAVID, in Strathmoir, 26 May 1770.

LUMSDEN, JAMES, mason in Cuminstown, 21 Apr 1786.

LUMSDEN, JEAN, Miss, daughter of late **Alexander L**, advocate in Aberdeen, 11 Dec 1784.

LUMSDEN, JEREMIAH, in Inverury, 31 Mar 1763.

LUMSDEN, JOHN, of Spring Garden, shipmaster in Aberdeen, 7 Jul 1774.

LUMSDEN, THOMAS, goldsmith in Aberdeen, 9 Jan 1773. See also **Katherine King**.

LUMSDEN, WILLIAM, in Meikle Rebra, 9 Sep 1772 and 14 Mar 1774.

LUNAN, ANDREW, glazier in Aberdeen. See Mrs **Catherine Hudart**.

LUNAN, JAMES, Mr, of Auchenlick, 23 May 1771.

LYON, JAMES, sometime at Slains Lodge, 15 Apr 1763.

McALLISTER, PETER, see **Peter McDonald**.

McCOMBIE, GEORGE, in Newbigging, 2 Nov 1786.

McCOMBIE, JAMES, blacksmith in Aberdeen, 7 Jun 1775.

McCONOCHIE, PETER, in Haugh of Edinglassie, 30 Sep 1771.

McDONALD, ALEXANDER, merchant in Aberdeen, 26 Jan 1773.

McDONALD, PETER, alias McALLISTER, mason in Aberdeen, 8 Jun 1775.

McFARLAN, ANDREW, son of late Capt **Duncan McF**, late of Lord Semple's Regiment, 17 Dec 1765.

McGIE, JOHN, see **Margaret Paterson**.

McGOWAN (or BALGOWAN), BESS, wife of **Robert Garrioch**, shoemaker, late in Gilcomston, now in Midmar, 14 Aug 1793.

McGREGOR, JAMES, alias GRIERSON, in Glengarden, 19 Dec 1778.

McGREGOR, JAMES, late at Pittyvaich, in parish of Mortlaich, 4 Jun 1790 and 2 Apr 1792.

McGREGOR, PETER, in Pittuthies, 13 Aug 1772.

McGREGOR, PETER, late in Clashenruich. See **Mary Stewart**.

McHARDIE, ALEXANDER, in Upper Tolduchoil, 18 Dec 1771.

McHARDIE, MARJORY, late in Burnside of Corriehoull, 15 Jul 1772.

McHARDIE, ROBERT, in Haugh of Cornlairg, in Glencluny, 20 Jun 1769.

MACHRAY, ALEXANDER, at Bridgefoot, parish of Cruden. See **Margaret Mowat**.

McINNES, NEIL, surveyor of windows, etc, in Aberdeen, 19 Dec 1792.

McINTOSH, JOHN, shoemaker in College Bounds of Old Aberdeen, 4 Oct 1766.

McINTOSH, JOHN, late at Mill of Corlarach, 22 Oct 1792.

McINTOSH, WILLIAM, in Cornalairg, in Glencluny, 18 Jun 1767.

MACKAY, KATHARINE, lately residing in Aberdeen, 19 Dec 1792.

MACKAY, WILLIAM, chapman in Fraserburgh, 13 Dec 1790.

MACKENZIE, BARBARA, Mrs, residing in Old Aberdeen, widow of **George Paton**, of Grandhome, 9 Jun 1789.

MACKENZIE, ELIZABETH, Mrs, formerly in Edinburgh, residing in Aberdeen, 17 Nov 1792.

MACKENZIE, JOHN, merchant in Aberdeen, 22 May 1764 and 1 Oct 1766.

MACKENZIE, JOHN, in Little Allnaquoich, 31 Jan 1771.

MACKENZIE, KENNETH, Mr, sometime in Braemar, thereafter in Aberdeen, 8 Mar 1776.

MACKENZIE, MARY, sometime in Park, parish of Lonmay, 26 Jan 1798.

MACKENZIE, WILLIAM, merchant in Aberdeen, 21 Jun 1766.

MACKENZIE, WILLIAM, in Kanakill, parish of Kindrought, 30 Oct 1778.

MACKIE, BARBARA, residing in Aberdeen, daughter of **William M**, at Gilcomstone, 10 Jul 1800.

MACKIE, JAMES, late of Gask, residing in Peterhead. See Mrs **Elizabeth Forbes**.

MACKIE, JOHN, late merchant in Aberdeen, 5 Sep 1772.

MACKIE, JOHN, late sergeant of the King's or 8th Regiment, thereafter residing in Aberdeen, 16 Sep 1785.

MACKIE, PATRICK, wright in Causeway. See **Anne Grant**.

MACKIE, ROBERT, in Upper Park of Drum, 13 Oct 1762.

MACKIE, SAMUEL, in Greens, 5 Mar 1771.

MACKIE, WILLIAM, in Tillyboa, parish of Kingedward, 20 Sep 1786.

MACKIE, WILLIAM, sometime mealseller in Aberdeen, 26 Apr 1787.

McLAGAN, WILLIAM, late in Falkirk, afterwards in Leyhead, parish of Tullich, 28 Feb 1794.

McLEOD, ALEXANDER, sometime in the service of East India Company, thereafter residing in Fraserburgh, 19 Nov 1793.

McLEOD, MARGARET, daughter of late **John McL**, sometime at Mill of Auchiries, and sometime wife of **William Thom**, in Fingask, 16 Jan 1795.

McPHERSON, JOHN, in Werdfold, 12 Mar 1798.

McPHERSON, NEIL, mariner in Aberdeen, 22 Jul 1791.

McQUEEN, LILLIAS, late cowfeeder in Old Aberdeen, 14 Jul 1789.

MACRAE, PETER, in Ferrar, 25 Feb 1760.

McROBB, JAMES, merchant in Redhill, 3 Apr 1766.

McWILLIAM, JAMES, Mr, late minister at Kildrummy, 4 Nov 1771.

McWILLIAM, ROBERT, in Achinhandock, 20 Sep 1763.

MAITLAND, ARTHUR, Major, of Pittrichie, 27 Mar 1768.

MAITLAND, JANET, widow of **William Milne**, late weaver in Aberdeen, 28 Jul 1790.

MAITLAND, MARY, in Pennyburn, 9 Jun 1766.

MALCOLM, JOHN, merchant in Aberdeen, 26 Feb 1789.

MARK, GEORGE, tailor in Aberdeen, 5 Dec 1766, see **Elizabeth Gordon**.

MARR, MARGARET, wife of **Patrick Taylor**, farmer in Cardrum, parish of Meldrum, 17 Nov 1778.

MARTIN, ALEXANDER, maltster in Aberdeen. See **Elizabeth Bartlet**.

MARTIN, JAMES, late in Glentown, 31 Jul 1770.

MARTIN, JOSEPH, chapman in Aberdeen, 29 Jun 1769.

MARTIN, WILLIAM, butcher in Aberdeen, 30 Nov 1797.

MASON, JOHN, see **Barbara Pirie**.

MASSON or MASON, ANN, residing in Aberdeen, widow of **James Brebner**, merchant in Aberdeen, 12 Jul 1792.

MASSON, WILLIAM, of Caldwells, parish of Ellon, sometime merchant in Aberdeen, 7 Apr 1791.

MASSIE, MARGARET, wife of **John Traill**, gardener in Aberdeen, 28 Feb 1771.

MASSIE, WILLIAM, in Cowhill, 10 Apr 1761.

MATHIESON, WILLIAM, in Edingarrock, 2 Jul 1772.

MAVOR, MARGARET, lately residing in Aberdeen, 9 Jul 1795.

MEDERS, JOHN, residing in Aberdeen, 21 Mar 1797.

MELDRUM, ANN, in Mains of Aberdour, widow of .... Wemyss, there, 19 Mar 1770.

MENNIE, JANET, wife of **George Herriegerrie** in Colpy, parish of Culsalmond, 7 Oct 1796.

MENNIE, WILLIAM, farmer at Countesswells, 21 Mar 1800.

MENNIE, ROBERT, burgess in Old Aberdeen, 22 Jun 1797.

MENZIES, JOHN, resident in Aberdeen, 9 Sep 1794.

MENZIES, JOHN, see **Ann Jessimin**.

MESTINE, JAMES, merchant in Aberdeen, 27 Mar 1764.

MICHIE, ELSPET, in Uppertoun of Glenbucket, 23 Dec 1783.

MICHIE, ROBERT, Mr, minister at Cluny, 25 Aug 1794 and 23 Jun 1795.

MIDDLETON, GEORGE, Esq, of Seaton, 1 Mar 1773.

MIDDLETON, JANET, Miss, daughter of late **William M**, of Sheils, sometime merchant in Aberdeen, 20 Aug 1799.

MIDDLETON, JOHN, merchant in Aberdeen, 2 Apr 1790.

MIDDLETON, WILLIAM, of Sheils, merchant in Aberdeen, 13 Nov 1760.

MIDDLETON, WILLIAM, sometime merchant in Aberdeen, 3 Feb and 9 Oct 1784. See also **Margaret Mitchell**.

MILLER, ALEXANDER, merchant in Banff, 16 Jul 1765.

MILLER, CHARLES, sometime cutler in London, thereafter residing in Aberdeen, 3 Dec 1790.

MILLER, JOHN, road contractor, lately residing in Aberdeen, 6 Sep 1798.

MILLISON, ALEXANDER, see **Lucretia Begg**.

MILNE, ALEXANDER, Esq, of Crimmondmogate, merchant in Aberdeen, 20 Nov 1789.

MILNE, ALEXANDER, shipmaster in Aberdeen, 3 Jun 1795.

MILNE, ELIZABETH, see **William Robertson**.

MILNE, GEORGE, Mr, in Woodhead, 20 Jun 1767.

MILNE, GEORGE, in Mains of Esslemont, 13 Jun 1795.

MILNE, ISOBEL, see **William Smith**.

MILNE, ISOBEL, in Middle Savock of Lonmay, 12 Jul 1790.

MILNE, JAMES, Mr, sometime Episcopal minister at Aberdeen. See **Elizabeth Skene**.

MILNE, JAMES, shipmaster in Aberdeen, 20 Jun 1769.

MILNE, JAMES, merchant in Aberdeen, 10 Jun 1777.

MILNE, JAMES, merchant at Newburgh, parish of Foveran, 12 Aug 1783.

MILNE, JAMES, in Ashalloch, 19 Jan 1786.

MILNE, JAMES, see **Isobel Cushnie**.

MILNE, JANET, late in Squairdoch, parish of Deskford, 26 May 1800.

MILNE, JEAN, in Little Wartler, 19 Nov 1782.

MILNE, JOHN, merchant in Aberdeen, 11 Oct 1800.

MILNE, MARGARET, widow of **Alexander Farquharson**, sometime in Burnroot, 15 Feb 1763.

MILNE, MARGARET, widow of Capt **Pember Britton**, late shipmaster at Aberdeen, now in Peterhead, 7 Aug 1770.

MILNE, MARGARET, Mrs, wife of .... **Gordon**, of Hopshill, 25 Nov 1784.

MITCHELL, MARGARET, see **John Osborne**.

MILNE, PATRICK, senior, merchant in Old Meldrum, 18 Mar 1796.

MILNE, THOMAS, sometime in Auchiries. See **Isobell Anderson**.

MILNE, WILLIAM, merchant in Seaton of Cairnbulg, 18 Apr 1777.

MILNE, WILLIAM, in Saak of Lonmay, 28 Sep 1789.

MILNE, WILLIAM, late weaver in Aberdeen. See **Janet Maitland**.

MITCHELL, ALEXANDER, merchant in Aberdeen, 25 Nov 1766 and 18 May 1767.

MITCHELL, ARTHUR, Mr, late minister at Skene, 13 Jul 1775.

MITCHELL, GEORGE, late merchant in Fraserburgh, 8 Jan 1790.

MITCHELL, JAMES, mariner in Aberdeen. See **Barbara Purse**.

MITCHELL, JAMES, late in New Balgowan of Keig, 7 Nov 1778.

MITCHELL, JOHN, sometime in Culhay, thereafter in Inch, 25 Mar 1762.

MITCHELL, JOHN, in Style of Tullich, 30 Aug 1773.

MITCHELL, JOHN, sometime in Foveran. See **Katharine Smith**.

MITCHELL, MARGARET, wife of **William Middleton**, merchant in Aberdeen, 7 and 13 July 1787.

MITCHELL, WILLIAM, merchant in Old Deer, 30 Nov 1768.

MITCHELL, WILLIAM, sometime in Mains of Artamford. See **Janet White**.

MOIR, ANDREW, tailor at Mill of Glenkindy, 20 Oct 1786.

MOIR, GEORGE, in Milltown of Durno, 28 Jan 1783.

MOIR, JAMES, of Invernettie, 18 Sep 1765.

MOIR, JAMES, see **Katharine Arbuthnot**.

MOIR, JAMES, late in Chapeltown, parish of Leslie, 19 Dec 1783.

MOIR, JOHN, in Aldie, 1 Dec 1795.

MOIR, ROBERT, merchant in Aberdeen, 30 Mar 1798.

MOIR, WILLIAM, advocate in Aberdeen, 13 Apr 1764.

MOLLISON, DAVID, sometime tailor in Lochtoun of Leys, 20 Feb 1777.

MONFORD, JOHN, see **Isobell Morice**.

MORE, JOHN, see **Janet Stephen**.

MORGAN, JAMES, in Millfield, parish of Leslie, 9 Mar 1772.

MORGAN, WILLIAM, Dr, late Rector of Kingston, Jamaica, and thereafter Professor of Philosophy in Marishall College of Aberdeen, 12 Feb 1789.

MORICE, ISOBELL, widow of **John Monfond**, late shipmaster in Aberdeen, 30 Jan 1792.

MORICE, JOHN, baker in Aberdeen, 18 Sep 1771.

MORICE, MARGARET, in Pitforskie, 2 Jun 1778.

MORISON, ALEXANDER, in Mains of Hatton, 3 Mar 1791.

MORISON, ELIZABETH, resident in Banff, widow of **George Gardner**, sometime in Blairshinnoch, 26 Jul 1775.

MORISON, ELSPET, resident in Banff, 2 Mar 1793.

MORISON, GEORGE, vintner in New Deer, 18 Dec (Aug) 1776.

MORISON, GEORGE, watchmaker in Aberdeen, 23 Jan 1792.

MORISON, JAMES, in Pitforskie, 11 Nov 1793.

MORISON, THOMAS, cooper in Fraserburgh, 27 Jun 1799.

MOWAT, ALEXANDER, Mr, minister at Foveran, 19 Jan 1775.

MOWAT, DAVID, shipmaster in Aberdeen, 30 Apr 1772.

MOWAT, ELSPET, widow of **James Day**, sometime sacrist in King's College of Aberdeen, 4 Feb 1789.

MOWAT, HELEN, sometime wife to **Nataniel Craig**, factor of Pitsligo, 7 Jun 1762.

MOWAT, JANET, in Burnside, Idoch, widow of **John Dent**, of Staindrop in Co of Durham, cheesemonger, 5 Jun 1797.

MOWAT, JOHN, late miller in Aberdeen, 29 Jul 1779.

MOWAT, MARGARET, late wife of **Alexander Machray**, of Bridgefoot, 13 Jun 1800.

MOWAT, WILLIAM, sometime merchant and provost of Aberdeen, afterwards residing at Newbridge, 4 Jul 1786 and 8 Feb 1787.

MUIR, JOHN, hookmaker in Cullen, 2 Jul 1762.

MUNRO, ALEXANDER, shoemaker at Denburn, near Aberdeen, 13 Nov 1783 and 3 May 1787.

MUNRO, WILLIAM, merchant in Banff, 16 Mar 1765.

MURRAY, ALEXANDER, late in Little Airdicaw, parish of Deskford, 5 Sep 1785.

MURRAY, ANDREW, in Gilcomston, 6 Feb 1770.

MURRAY, ANDREW, sometime in Mayen, thereafter in Gilcomston, 17 Feb 1791.

MURRAY, DAVID, sometime in Broadtack of Elrick, late in Kinmundy of New Machar. See **Christian Mutch**.

MURRAY, ELIZABETH, daughter of late **John M**, brewer in Canongate, and wife of **Lewis Murray**, innkeeper at Pockraw of Aberdeen, 26 Jun 1778.

MURRAY, JAMES, merchant in Fraserburgh, 14 Apr 1760.

MURRAY, JAMES, thread dyer in Aberdeen, 27 Nov 1793.

MURRAY, JOHN, sometime of the Island of Demerara, lately residing at Portsoy, 2 Jul 1795.

MURRAY, LEWIS, vintner at Blockhouse of Aberdeen, 22 May 1782.

MURRAY, LEWIS, see **Elizabeth Murray**.

MURRAY, WILLIAM, late servant to Charles Gordon of Abergeldie, 29 May 1777.

MURRAY, WILLIAM, merchant in Aberdeen, 2 Jun 1792.

MURRIAN, PETER, in Craigingower of Glenbucket, 23 Dec 1783.

MURTRAE, GEORGE, late merchant in Banff, 12 Aug 1784 and 21 Feb 1785.

MUTCH, CHRISTIAN, widow of **David Murray**, sometime in Broadtack of Elrick, late in Kinundy of New Machar, 4 May 1787.

MUTCHE, GEORGE, sometime in New Deer, 5 Aug 1789.

NAIRN, MARGARET, see **John Smith**.

NAPIER, ARCHIBALD, Mr, late minister at Maryculter, 24 Jun 1762.

NAUGHTIE, JAMES, miller at Gilcomstone, 9 Jan 1777.

NEILSON, WILLIAM, deacon, butcher in Aberdeen, 21 May 1785.

NICOL, ALEXANDER, late in Middletoun of Balquhain, 26 Nov 1776.

NICOL, ALEXANDER, maltster in Aberdeen, 9 Sep 1794.

NICOL, JOHN, merchant in Aberdeen, 28 Apr 1794.

NICOL, WILLIAM, in Clerkhill, parish of Peterhead, 8 Jan 1767.

NICOL, WILLIAM, advocate in Aberdeen, 30 Jun 1789.

NICOLSON, AMELIA, Mrs, widow of Mr **James Dunbar**, minister at Boyndie, 20 Dec 1785.

NICOLSON, JAMES, Mr, minister at Nether Banchory, 19 Dec 1774 and 22 Feb 1776.

NICOLSON, JOHN, late in Auchterless. See **Isobel Skene**.

NORTON, CHRISTOPHER, formerly of Reading, Co Berks, gentleman, lately residing at Tomley, Co Aberdeen, 26 May 1800.

OGG, JOHN, merchant in Banff, 26 Jun and 28 Oct 1760.

OGILVIE, ALEXANDER, in Tochineal or Cullen, 13 Apr 1798.

OGILVIE, GRIZEL, eldest daughter and heir of Mr **John O**, of Balbegno, advocate, widow of Dr **John Brisbane**, sometime physician in London, 2 Aug 1785 and 12 Jul 1787.

OGILVIE, ISOBEL, Mrs, otherwise **Duff**, residing in the town of Macduff, 12 Jun 1798.

OGILVIE, JAMES, at Letterfury, 13 Aug 1774.

OGILVIE, MARY, Mrs, widow of **John Joss**, of Collinart, 30 May 1789.

OGILVIE, WILLIAM, merchant in Aberdeen, 19 Sep 1760.

OGILVIE, WILLIAM, merchant in Banff, 14 Mar 1788.

OGSTON, ALEXANDER, tidewaiter in Fraserburgh, 4 Jun 1781.

OGSTON, JOHN, in Mains of Arnage, 30 Jul 1771.

OGSTON, MARTHA, late residing in Aberdeen, 31 May 1791.

OLIPHANT, ALEXANDER, in Oldmad, 22 Mar 1771.

OLIPHANT, MARGARET, in Knaven, widow of **Andrew Crichton**, late in parish of Fyvie, 12 Oct 1790.

ORCHERTON, ISOBEL, see **George Low**.

ORD, ELSPET, widow of **James Abercrombie**, bailie of Cullen, 28 Apr 1762.

OSBURN, ALEXANDER, comptroller of Customs at Port of Aberdeen, 10 Jun 1785.

OSBURN, JOHN, Mr, minister at Aberdeen and Principal of Marishall College there. See **Margaret Mitchell**.

PANTON, ADAM, see **Sarah Wood**.

PANTON, ALEXANDER, merchant in Turriff, 19 Aug 1751 and 18 Feb 1762.

PANTON, GEORGE, see **Isabel Dickie**.

PANTON, WILLIAM, late in Burnside of Endach, 18 Aug 1777.

PATERSON, ALEXANDER, late merchant in Banff, 15 Dec 1775 and 6 Mar 1777.

PATERSON, ELLIOT, Miss, residing in Aberdeen, eldest daughter of late **John P**, 13 Jul 1786.

PATERSON, JAMES, in Tarves, 22 Feb 1763.

PATERSON, JANE, late in Peterhead, widow of **Joseph Johnston**, sometime quartermaster in 10th Regiment of Foot, 11 Oct 1779.

PATERSON, MARGARET, widow of **John McGie**, late surgeon apothecary in Aberdeen, 5 Oct 1763.

PATERSON, ROBERT, sometime in Upper Foulis of Craigievar, thereafter tanner in Aberdeen, 28 Oct 1793.

PATERSON, WALTER, in Springfield, 20 Jun 1772.

PATERSON, WILLIAM, late in Coldwells, 10 Jan 1775.

PATON, GEORGE, see **Barbara Mackenzie**.

PATON, ISOBELLA, Miss, daughter of **John P**, Esq, of Grandhome, 30 May 1778.

PAUL, ANN, widow of **John Hope**, resident in Aberdeen, 12 Mar 1790.

PAUL, ANDREW, see **Susanna Paul**.

PAUL, SUSANNA, Mrs, widow of Mr **Andrew P**, residing in Aberdeen, 18 Jun 1798.

PEAT, JAMES, collector of Excise in Aberdeen, 23 Sep 1797.

PETERKIN, JAMES, in Newmills of Boyne, 20 Aug 1772.

PETRIE, ARTHUR, resident in Aberdeen, 4 Feb 1788.

PETRIE, JAMES, advocate in Aberdeen, 30 Nov 1763 and 19 Jul 1764.

PETRIE, JAMES, in Kirktoun Mill, parish of Drumblate, 6 Dec 1781.

PHILIP, GEORGE, Bailie and merchant in Banff. See Mrs **Elizabeth Forbes**.

PHILIP, WILLIAM, late in Muirton of Barra, 3 Aug 1790.

PHILP alias PHILIPS, JOHN, son of **John P**, alias P, whitefisher in Ward of Ardendraught, sailor on board the *Terpsichore* man-of-war, 2 Dec 1762.

PHILP, JOHN, mariner in Aberdeen, 10 Aug 1784.

PIRIE, ALEXANDER, in Westertoun of Pitfoddles, 18 Jul 1776.

PIRIE, ANDREW, sometime in Cortans, 29 Apr 1763.

PIRIE, BARBARA, widow of **John Mason**, merchant in Aberdeen, 1 Jun 1762.

PIRIE, JANET, late in Cloak, 12 Nov 1790.

PIRIE, PATRICK, merchant in Aberdeen, 22 Jun 1787.

PIRIE, PATRICK, sometime merchant in Aberdeen, 21 Feb 1793.

PIRIE, WILLIAM, servant to Harry Watson in Mill of Fintray, 26 Sep 1797.

PITTENDREICH, MARY, at Nether Kinmundy, parish of Longside, daughter of **James P**, gardener or nurseryman in Longside, 21 May 1793.

PORTER, MARJORY or MAY, sometime resident in Footdee, 29 Jul 1794.

PRATT, MARGARET, wife of **James Hay**, dyer at Bridgend of Fyvie, 23 Nov 1764.

PRINGLE, JEAN, Mrs, daughter of the late **Walter P**, of Craigcrook, advocate, 5 Jan 1762.

PROCTOR, GEORGE, butcher in Aberdeen, 1 Feb 1774.

PROTT, WILLIAM, late sailor in Portsoy, 18 Oct 1784.

PURDIE, JOHN, merchant in Aberdeen, 15 Feb and 4 Jul 1785.

PURSE, BARBARA, wife to **James Mitchell**, mariner in Aberdeen, 30 Sep 1769.

PYPER, WILLIAM, stockingmaker in Brae of Pitfoddels, 5 Apr 1791.

RAE, MARGARET, see **George Couts.**

RAGG, HELEN, daughter of late **Robert R**, shipmaster in Aberdeen, 24 Jul 1781.

RAINY, JAMES, in Mains of Dummuie, 7 Jan 1775.

RAINY, JOHN, sometime merchant, thereafter post in Fraserburgh, 16 May 1778.

RAINY, JOHN, sometime in Machan, theeafter in Turriff, 29 Dec 1778.

RAINY, JOHN, shipmaster in Aberdeen, 3 Nov 1800.

RAINY, WILLIAM, in Begshill, parish of Drumblade, 15 Nov 1798.

RAMSAY, ALEXANDER, merchant in Roseharty, and **Barbara R**, there, his sister, 4 Dec 1792.

RAMSAY, ALEXANDER, sometime vintner in Old Meldrum. See **Elspet Thomson**.

RAMSAY, BARBARA, see **Alexander Ramsay**.

RAMSAY, DAVID, lately residing in Aberdeen, 4 May 1789.

RAMSAY, JAMES, advocate in Aberdeen, 16 May 1775, 1 Aug 1776 and 18 and 21 Jun 1777.

RAMSAY, JOHN, of Barra, 21 Dec 1787.

RANKIN, WILLIAM, in Pirscow, 11 Aug 1779.

RATTRAY, DAVID, see **Margaret Wilson**.

REID, ALEXANDER, in Kinbeam, and **George R**, his only child, 1 Oct 1762.

REID, ALEXANDER, Mr, minister at Kemnay, 12 Aug 1782.

REID, ALEXANDER, flaxdresser in Aberdeen, 27 Aug 1799.

ARCHIBALD REID, see **Jean Crombie**.

REID, CHARLES, in Bodom, parish of Insh, 5 Dec 1765.

REID, CHARLES, shipmaster in Fraserburgh, 24 Mar 1789.

REID, COSMO, late in Restonhillock, 3 May 1771 and 8 Apr 1773.

REID, GEORGE, see **Alexander Reid**.

REID, ISABEL, in Upper Drumalachy, 21 Dec 1799.

REID, JAMES, sometime at Slains Castle, in parish of Slains, 31 May 1788.

REID, JAMES, late in Tornaveen, 1 Sep 1791.

REID, JAMES, sometime in Wauchandale of Echt, afterwards residing in Aberdeen, 18 Dec 1793.

REID, JANET, resident in Aberdeen, 14 Jul 1761.

REID, JANET, widow of **Alexander Duncan**, junior, merchant in Aberdeen, 21 Jun 1773.

REID, JEAN, daughter of **Robert R**, farmer in Dub Castle, 25 Nov 1776.

REID, RACHEL, in Tirrivaill of Skene, 6 May 1762.

REID, PETER, formerly merchant in Aberdeen, landwaiter of the Customs there, 27 Jun 1775.

REID, PETER, sometime of Leys, and afterwards in Kinclean, 24 Jan 1785.

REID, ROBERT, see **Jean Reid**.

REID, THOMAS, Mr, minister at Leochell, 16 Jun 1772.

REID, WILLIAM, late merchant in New Deer, 7 May 1790.

REID, WILLIAM, sometime shipmaster in Peterhead, 14 Dec 1792.

RETTIE, JANET, sometime in Broomhill, parish of New Deer, 11 May 1799.

RIACH, DUNCAN, blacksmith in Old Aberdeen. See **Marjory Tholson**.

RIACH, PETER, in Bellamore, 20 Jun 1792.

RICHARDSON, GEORGE, in Tukes, parish of Old Deer, 24 Jan 1775.

RICKART, HELEN, widow of **John Cordoner,** in Old Deer, 29 Apr 1774.

RIDDELL, ANDREW, see **Helen Farquhar**.

RIDDOCH, CHRISTIAN, Miss, daughter of Mr **James R**, minister in St Paul's Chapel, Aberdeen, 7 Jan 1779.

RIDDOCH, JAMES, Mr, see **Christian Riddoch**.

RITCHIE, ALEXANDER, late in Tamantum, 8 Jan 1760.

RITCHIE, HECTOR, late in Old Overtoun, thereafter in Old Aberdeen, 28 Feb 1792.

RITCHIE, JAMES, sometime in Kintocher, parish of Lumphanan. See **Elspet Walker**.

RITCHIE, THOMAS, mariner in Aberdeen, 24 Oct 1761.

ROBB, ISABELLA, Mrs, in Nether Kinmundy, 29 Nov 1792.

ROBB, JOHN, late in Haddo, 19 Nov 1788.

ROBB, MAY, resident in Aberdeen, 16 Sep 1788.

ROBERTSON, ALEXANDER, in Boghead, 9 May 1763.

ROBERTSON, ALEXANDER, Mr, minister at Longside, 18 Jun 1764.

ROBERTSON, ALEXANDER, merchant in Aberdeen, 25 Jun 1765.

ROBERTSON, ALEXANDER, merchant in Fraserburgh, 11 Dec 1767.

ROBERTSON, ALEXANDER, Provost of Glasgowego. See Mrs **Jean Rose**.

ROBERTSON, ALEXANDER, lately residing in London, thereafter at Craigellie, 11 Aug 1787.

ROBERTSON, ALEXANDER, sometime merchant in Portsoy, 8 Jun 1791.

ROBERTSON, ALEXANDER, of Blackchambers, 8 Nov 1793.

ROBERTSON, ALEXANDER, see **Christian Clark**.

ROBERTSON, ARTHUR, surgeon in Old Meldrum. See Dame **Katharine Stewart**.

ROBERTSON, CHARLES, residing in Aberdeen, brother-german of late **Isaac R**, mill carpenter on Richmond Estate, parish of St George and Island of Grenada, 5 Oct 1791.

ROBERTSON, GEORGE, junior, merchant in Portsoy, 25 May 1781.

ROBERTSON, GEORGE, sometime in Boddoms, parish of New Machar, 29 Jul 1794.

ROBERTSON, ISAAC, see **Charles Robertson**.

ROBERTSON, JAMES, junior, merchant in Portsoy, 25 May 1781.

ROBERTSON, JAMES, merchant in Roseharty, 13 Feb 1794.

ROBERTSON, MARGARET, resident in Aberdeen, 20 Jan 1770.

ROBERTSON, MARJORY, wife of **Thomas Davidson**, in Whitehouse Croft, near Aberdeen, 1 Aug 1771.

ROBERTSON, WILLIAM, farmer in Stodley, and **Elizabeth Milne**, his widow, 20 Mar 1765.

ROBERTSON, WILLIAM, sometime in Inver of Monymusk, 17 Dec 1796.

ROBSON, JOHN, sometime in Lasts. See **Jean Keillo**.

ROGER, CATHERINE, residing in Aberdeen, daughter of late **Janet Donald**, widow of **John Roger**, sometime residing in Aberdeen, 19 Jan 1797.

ROGER, JOHN, see **Catherine Roger** and **Janet Donald**.

ROLLAND, MARGARET, lately residing in Pitfoddles, widow of **George Duncan**, sometime merchant in Aberdeen, 31 Jul 1776.

ROSE, ANNE, widow of **George Lobban**, sometime landwaiter in Aberdeen, 10 Mar 1795.

ROSE, DAVID, sometime quarrier in Aberdeen, 23 Mar 1773.

ROSE, JAMES, of Clava, 3 Mar 1774.

ROSE, JEAN, Mrs, widow of Provost **Alexander Robertson**, of Glasgowego, 8 Oct 1784.

ROSS, ALEXANDER, junior, merchant in Aberdeen, 6 Feb 1784.

ROSS, ALEXANDER, in Blackhills, 20 Jul and 14 Nov 1775.

ROSS, ALEXANDER, in Blackhills of Montquhiter, 23 Jun 1778.

ROSS, ANN. See **Patrick Souper**.

ROSS, CHRISTIAN, see **Arthur Forbes**.

ROSS, EUPHAN, at Hazelhead, 11 Aug 1775.

ROSS, FRANCIS, surgeon in Old Meldrum, 17 Jan 1771.

ROSS, HUGH, see **Francis Ross**.

ROSS, JEAN, see **Alexander Aberdeen.**

ROSS, JOHN, in Ennachy, 6 Mar 1761.

ROSS, JOHN, in Mill of Lernie, 9 Jul 1761.

ROSS, JOHH, merchant in Aberdeen, 4 Mar 1788.

ROSS, PETER, mason in Aberdeen, 26 May 1800.

ROSS, WILLIAM, in Brownie, parish of Durris, 14 Jun 1784.

ROSS, WILLIAM, sometime soldier in the 47th Regiment of Foot, last residing in Banff, 18 Apr 1788.

ROUGH, HELEN, resident in Aberdeen, 8 Apr 1790.

ROUST, JOHN, carter in Windmill brae of Aberdeen, 22 May 1789.

ROY, ANDREW, merchant in Aberdeen, 29 Jul 1777.

ROY, JEAN, residing in Aberdeen, 17 Feb 1791.

ROY, JOHN, lately residing in Laichie of Mortlach, 24 Sep 1795.

RUDDACH, GEORGE, late vintner in Portsoy, 15 Nov 1788.

RUDDIMAN, JOHN, in Clayfolds, 12 Oct 1770.

RUGLAN, JAMES, weaver in Old Rain, 20 Nov 1795.

RUNCIE, ALEXANDER, tenant in Briach, 29 Oct 1777.

RUNCIE, JOHN, Capt, shipmaster in Down, 17 Mar 1786.

RUSSELL, JOHN, of Raithen, sometime merchant in Banff, 27 Feb 1766.

SALTON, GEORGE, Lord, 24 Aug 1782.

SANDILANDS, ELIZABETH, Mrs, sister-german to **Robert S**, of Wester Arachies, 12 Jun 1777.

SANDILANDS, PATRICK, Esq, late merchant in Aberdeen, 23 Feb 1797.
SANDILANDS, ROBERT, of Wester Draikies, advocate in Aberdeen, 14 Jan 1775.
SANDILANDS, ROBERT, see **Elizabeth Sandilands**.
SANDISON, GEORGE, late tenant in Petts, 31 Jul 1783.
SANDISON, ROBERT, Excise Officer in Aberdeen, 25 Jun 1790.
SANGSTER, MARGARET, in Kintore, widow of **William Stewart**, vintner there, 13 Aug 1782.
SANGSTER, PATRICK, sometime shipmaster in Gardenstoun, and Commander of the sloop *Happy Return*, 19 Apr 1773.
SANGSTER, WILLIAM, in Mill of Wardhouse. See **Janet Stephen**.
SAUNDERS, JAMES, Dr, physician in Banff, 20 Sept 1779.
SCORGIE, JANET, residing in Fraserburgh, 17 May 1796.
SCOTT, ALEXANDER, maltster, burgess of Aberdeen, 5 Aug 1763.
SCOTT, ALEXANDER, wright, burgess of Aberdeen, 22 Aug 1787.
SCOTT, GEORGE, late at Mill of Aden, 19 Dec 1789.
SCOTT, GRIZEL, widow of **John Kidd**, in Rora, 31 Dec 1766.
SCOTT, JAMES, late gardener at Logie, 9 Sep 1797.
SCOTT, JAMES, sometime farmer in Boghadlie. See **Ann Hog**.
SCOTT, JOHN, late in Lumbs, 20 Dec 1792.
SCOTT, WILLIAM, lately residing in Aberdeen, and late Commander of the *Prince Earnest Augustine*, cutter in employ of HM Customs, 27 Jun and 5 Oct 1787.
SCOTT, WILLIAM, in Mains of Brucklaw, 15 Nov 1798 and 3 Apr 1800.
SCOTT, WILLIAM, sometime watchmaker in London, afterwards of Fallside, and thereafter residing in Hardgate of Aberdeen, 22 Nov 1798.
SCROGGS, ALEXANDER, farmer at Bridge of Don, 21 Dec 1769.
SCROGGS, JOHN, sometime merchant in Aberdeen, 28 Jul 1790.
SETON or SEATON, ELSPET, widow of **John Smith**, merchant in Gallowgate of Aberdeen, 26 Feb 1782.
SETON, JOHN, residing at Whitside of Rathven, 10 May 1791.
SETON, WILLIAM, Sir, of Pitmedden, Bart, 8 May 1775.
SHAND, GEORGE, late in Aberdeen, sometime in Demerara. See **Mary Walker**.
SHAND, JAMES, junior, merchant in Banff, 16 Jul 1765.
SHAND, JOHN, late in Muirton of Forgue, 19 Jun 1770.
SHAW, ALEXANDER, youngest son of late **James S**, of Daldownie, 3 Dec 1772.
SHAW, JAMES, see **Alexander Shaw**.
SHAW, JOHN, in Ellon, 19 Aug 1771.

SHEARER, ALEXANDER, sometime in Breda, parish of Alford, youngest son of late **Thomas S**, sometime in Creach, parish of Auchindore, 21 Jul 1785 and 14 Mar 1786.

SHEARER, THOMAS, see **Alexander Shearer**.

SHEPHERD, DANIEL, in Miln of Barns, 1 Aug 1767.

SHEPHERD, MARGARET, widow of **Francis Daunay**, factor on the Estate of Haughton, 30 Mar 1785.

SHEPHERD, MARGARET, widow of **David Gill**, shoemaker in Aberdeen, 25 Feb 1796.

SHEPHERD, THOMAS, cooper in Aberdeen, 29 Jan 1783.

SHEPHERD, WILLIAM, shoemaker in Aberdeen, 17 Feb 1763.

SHERRIFF, ALEXANDER, merchant in Aberdeen, 4 Jul 1793.

SHERRIFF, JAMES, tenant in Midtoun of Badenspink, 28 Dec 1764.

SHINIE, ALEXANDER, soapmaker in Aberdeen, 11 Feb 1783.

SHIRRAS, BARBARA, widow of **Robert Brebner**, in Hilltown, 30 Dec 1799.

SHIRRAS, MARY, niece of **Alexander Gordon**, merchant in Boulogne-sur-la-mer in France, and wife of **Alexander Farquhar**, late in Westoun, thereafter in Gilcomston, 7 Oct 1774.

SHIVAS, ALEXANDER, younger, late in Nether Tocher, 22 Oct 1774.

SHIVAS, ANDREW, vintner in Peterhead, 19 Mar 1795.

SILVER, WILLIAM, shipmaster in Aberdeen, 17 Apr 1761.

SIMPSON, ALEXANDER, of Concraig, 22 Jun 1768 and 18 May (Jan) 1769.

SIMPSON, ALEXANDER, Mr, minister at Monymusk, 21 May 1781.

SIMPSON, ALEXANDER, cashier of the Aberdeen Banking Co, 28 Feb 1794.

SIMPSON, GEORGE, tailor in Aberdeen, 12 Jul 1763.

SIMPSON, JANET, wife of **Alexander Garden**, workman in Aberdeen, 28 Jan 1782.

SIMPSON, PATRICK, of Conersig, 18 Jun 1763.

SIMPSON, PETER, late merchant in Aberdeen, 19 Nov 1800.

SIMPSON, ROBERT, of Thornton, 29 Mar 1773.

SIMPSON, WILLIAM, feuar of Ferryhill, sometime merchant in Aberdeen, 27 Dec 1766.

SINGER, ADAM, at Mill of Glanderston, 27 Apr 1790.

SINGER, ADAM, merchant in Aberdeen, 31 Dec 1799.

SINGER, WILLIAM, in Belthelney, 27 Feb 1776.

SKENE, ANDREW, Mr, minister at Banff, 17 May 1793.

SKENE, ELIZABETH, widow of Mr **James Milne**, sometime Episcopal minister in Aberdeen, 29 Dec 1762.

SKENE, ISOBEL, widow of **John Nicolson**, late in Auchterless, 29 Jun 1792.

SKENE, JAMES, Capt, Aberdeen, late of 98th Regiment of Foot, 3 Nov 1797.

SKENE, KATHARINE, widow of **Alexander Thomson**, of Banchory, 10 Mar 1778.

SKENE, THOMAS, sometime residing at Scotstoun, afterwards at Bridge of Don, 23 Aug 1799.

SKINNER, JOHN, Mr, schoolmaster of Echt, 4 Feb 1777.

SKINNER, ROBERT, late mason in Lemless, parish of Aberdour, 20 Dec 1776.

SMITH, ALEXANDER, in Kingshill of Counteswells, 28 Apr and 2 Dec 1749, 13 Mar 1759 and 29 May 1760.

SMITH, ALEXANDER, late in Rora, 17 Dec 1778.

SMITH, ALEXANDER, in Woodend, 8 Feb 1800.

SMITH, ANN, sometime in Milnbowie. See **James Thomson**.

SMITH, GEORGE, sometime shipmaster at Fraserburgh, 13 Feb 1770.

SMITH, GEORGE, late of Broomhill, lately residing in Aberdeen, 25 Nov 1799.

SMITH, JAMES, in Cordshill, 27 Jun 1766.

SMITH, JOHN, see **Elspet Seton**.

SMITH, JOHN, in Auchmore, 10 Nov 1765.

SMITH, JOHN, blacksmith and convener in Old Aberdeen, and **Christian Chalmers**, his wife, 18 Apr 1772.

SMITH, JOHN, mason in Aberdeen, 24 Dec 1778.

SMITH, JOHN, in Auchmore, parish of Mortlick, and **Margaret Nairn**, his wife, 29 Jun 1786.

SMITH, JOHN, late of Antigua, thereafter residing at Cherryvale, near Aberdeen, 9 Jul 1795.

SMITH, JOHN, weaver in Gilcomston, 26 Dec 1796.

SMITH, JOHN, pewterer and auctioneer in Aberdeen, 18 Sep 1799.

SMITH, JOHN, youngest, merchant in Aberdeen, 14 May 1800.

SMITH, KATHARINE, residing in Aberdeen, widow of **John Mitchell**, sometime in Foveran, 4 Jul 1794.

SMITH, PATRICK, blacksmith in Banff, 12 Jun 1781.

SMITH, PETER, late dyer in Gilcomston, 6 Jun 1776.

SMITH, WILLIAM, convener of tailors in Aberdeen, 1 Aug 1763.

SMITH, WILLIAM, junior, merchant in Aberdeen, 30 Jan 1796.

SMITH, WILLIAM, see **Isobel Milne**.

SMITH, WILLIAM, Mr, see **Mary Turner**.

SNAWIE, WILLIAM, servant to Mr John Glenny, minister at Maryculter, 3 Jun 1768.

SOMERVILLE, JEAN, widow of **Archibald Stewart**, late supervisor of Excise at Ellon, 7 Oct 1763.

SOUPER, PATRICK, merchant in Aberdeen, and **Ann Ross**, his wife, 12 Oct 1775.

SOUTER, JAMES, merchant in Peterhead, 15 Dec 1774.

SPALDING, PETER, late farm servant at Culter, 6 Mar 1795.

SPENCE, JOHN, in Easter Buckett, 15 Nov 1768.

STABLES, CHRISTIAN, see **Helen Stables**.

STEPHEN or STEVEN, ALEXANDER, in Farmtown of Balfluig, 30 Jul 1800.

STEPHEN, ANN, late in Hardward, near Aberdeen, 9 Dec 1775.

STEPHEN, GEORGE, in Bonnytown, 9 Feb 1678.

STEPHEN, GEORGE, in Bonnytown, eldest son of **George S**, sometime in Bonnytoun, 20 Nov 1788.

STEPHEN, GEORGE, late at Cairnery, parish of Old Macher, 29 Jan 1798.

STEPHEN, GEORGE, see **James Stephen**.

STEPHEN, GEORGE, Mr, see **James Stephen**.

STEPHEN, HELEN, wife to **George Barron**, tailor in Old Govall, 30 Jul 1781.

STEPHEN, JAMES, in Mill of Pitmedden, son of Mr **George Stephen**, sometime of Glennieston, 17 Jul 1772.

STEPHEN, JAMES, sometime blacksmith in Old Meldrum, 10 Aug 1781.

STEPHEN, JANET, sometime wife to **William Sangster**, in Mill of Wardhouse, now wife of **John More**, late in Glenniestoun, now in Ladiken, 20 Jan 1762.

STEPHEN, JEAN, sometime wife of **Alexander Black**, gardener in Aberdeen, 1 Aug 1789.

STEPHEN, JOHN, in Fisherford, 14 Apr 1774.

STEPHEN, RACHEL, wife of **James Deans**, merchant in Old Meldrum, 22 Aug 1794.

STEPHEN, ROBERT, merchant in Aberdeen, 29 Aug 1741, 15 Dec 1742 and 23 Oct 1761.

STEVENSON or STEPHENSON, DAVID, Mr, minister at Pitsligo, 22 Mar 1787.

STEWART, ALEXANDER, merchant in Aberdeen, 11 Mar 1766.

STEWART, ARCHIBALD, supervisor of Excise at Ellon, 29 Dec 1757, 26 Dec 1758 and 29 Jun 1764. See also **Jean Somerville**.

STEWART, DAVID, Mr, physician in Aberdeen, 28 Aug 1786.

STEWART, ISABELL, see **James Grant**.

STEWART, JEAN, daughter of Mr **Walter S**, minister at Ellon, 30 Sep 1771.

STEWART, JOHN, Mr, Professor of Mathematics in the Marishall College of Aberdeen, 20 Dec 1766.

STEWART, JOHN, late in Crofts of Glenbucket, 20 Nov 1778.

STEWART, JOHN, shipmaster in Aberdeen, 4 Aug 1795.

STEWART, KATHARINE, Dame, widow of **Arthur Robertson**, surgeon in Old Meldrum, and daughter of Mr **Walter S**, minister at Ellon, 30 Sep 1771.

STEWART, MARGARET, widow of **Charles Gordon**, of Fetterangus, daughter of Mr **Walter S**, minister at Ellon, 30 Sep 1771.

STEWART, MARGARET, see **William Farquharson**.

STEWART, MARY, late in Strathgirnoch, widow of **Peter McGregor**, late in Clashinruich, 8 Mar 1785.

STEWART, PETER, late in Nether Cluny, parish of Mortlach, 26 Feb 1790.

STEWART, ROBERT, at Mill of Stirren, 29 Nov 1768.

STEWART, THOMAS JOHN, surgeon in Kincardin O'Neil, 23 May (12 Jan) 1797.

STEWART, WALTER, Mr, see **Jean Stewart**, and Dame **Katharine Stewart**.

STEWART, WILLIAM, vintner in Kintore. See **Margaret Sangster**.

STILL, ALEXANDER, junior, butcher in Aberdeen, 15 Jul 1783.

STILL, GEORGE, merchant in Aberdeen, 20 Sep 1779.

STILL, GEORGE, shipmaster in Aberdeen, 1 Sep 1800.

STILL, ISOBELL, widow of **James Beverly**, sometime farmer in Lochhills, lately residing in Old Aberdeen, 19 Nov 1767.

STILL, JOHN, see **Isobell Duncan**.

STILLAS, ALEXANDER, late merchant in Old Meldrum, 31 Aug 1790.

STRACHAN, ALEXANDER, miller in Aberdeen, and **Janet Cruikshank**, his wife, 13 Jul 1761.

STRACHAN, ALEXANDER, Dr, physician in Banff, 12 Aug 1763.

STRACHAN, ALEXANDER, Mr, minister at Keig, 16 Dec 1771. See also **Elizabeth Wilson**.

STRACHAN, BARBARA, daughter of late **Robert S**, of Tillyfour, 29 Oct 1762.

STRACHAN, INNES, Mr, minister at Kinkell, 21 Jan 1762 and 20 Apr 1767.

STRACHAN, JOHN, see **William Strachan**.

STRACHAN, ROBERT, see **Barbara Strachan**.

STRACHAN, WILLIAM, sometime merchant in Rotterdam, last residing in Banff, 22 Jul 1777.

SUTHERLAND, ALEXANDER, see Mrs **Elizabeth Sutherland**.

SUTHERLAND, ELIZABETH, Mrs, daughter of **Alexander S**, of Kinminity, 15 Jun 1786.

SUTHERLAND, WILLIAM S, late merchant in Thurso, 3 May and 21 Dec 1798.

SYME or SYM, ALEXANDER, late in Auchines, parish of Rathven, 23 Feb 1792.

SYME, ANDREW, merchant in Aberdeen, 26 May 1780.

SYME, GEORGE, late in Overhill, parish of Tarves, 18 Nov 1794.

SYME, WALTER, Mr, late minister at Tillinessle, see **Barbara Calder**.

SYME, WALTER, Mr, sometime minister at Mortlick, 1 Mar 1763.

SYMMER, GEORGE, Capt, late of HM 25th Regiment of Foot, and barrackmaster in Aberdeen, 4 May 1796.

TAES, WALTER, shipmaster in Peterhead, 20 Jun 1783.

TARRAS, DAVID, resident in Peterhead, 27 Dec 1765.

TAWS or TAUSE, ELIZABETH, resident in Aberdeen, widow of **Gilbert Fergus**, tailor in Glasgow, 20 Mar (Apr) 1770.

TAWS, JOHN, customer at Tarland, 21 Dec 1782.

TAYLOR, ALEXANDER, at Haddowhouse, thereafter residing in Aberdeen, 27 Sep 1791.

TAYLOR, JOHN, advocate in Aberdeen, 3 Dec 1788.

TAYLOR, PATRICK, farmer in Cardrum, parish of Meldrum. See also **Margaret Marr**.

TAYLOR, ROBERT, wright in Aberdeen, 6 Mar 1783.

TAYLOR, WILLIAM, in Roundlight Knot, 8 Feb 1787.

TAYLOR, WILLIAM, clerk to late **James Burnet**, merchant in Aberdeen, 14 Jul 1789.

TAYLOR, WILLIAM, late merchant in Peterhead, 20 Aug 1795.

TAYLOR, WILLIAM, Mr, minister at New Deer, 19 Feb 1800.

TEMPLE, ELSPET or ELIZABETH, resident in Aberdeen, 3 Jun 1791.

TESTARD, JAMES, late in Luidmuic of Glenmuick, 29 Oct 1800.

THAIN, ELIZABETH, second daughter of late Mr **William T**, of Blackhall, wife to Mr **Thomas Cruikshank**, merchant in Aberdeen, 2 Sep 1762.

THAIN, WILLIAM, see **Elizabeth Thain**.

THAW, JAMES, in Tillyfroskie, 30 Oct 1789.

THOLSON, MARJORY, widow of **Duncan Riach**, blacksmith in Old Aberdeen, thereafter wife to **Arthur Glenny**, wright at Causeway, 16 Oct 1769.

THOM, ALEXANDER, in Old Westhall, 7 Jan 1774.

THOM, WILLIAM, Dr, advocate in Aberdeen, 20 May 1797.

THOM, WILLIAM, see **Margaret McLeod**.

THOMSON, ALEXANDER, see **Katharine Skene**.

THOMSON, ALEXANDER, shoemaker in Aberdeen, 31 Jan 1760.

THOMSON, ANDREW, advocate in Aberdeen, 27 Jul 1767.

THOMSON, ANDREW, see **Margaret Thomson**.

THOMSON, ELSPET, lately residing at Kingswells, widow of **Alexander Ramsay**, sometime vintner in Old Meldrum, 7 Mar 1797.

THOMSON, JAMES, in Milnbowie, and **Ann Smith**, his wife, sometime there, thereafter in Meikletoun of Crabstone, 14 Mar 1769.

THOMSON, JAMES, student of physick, only child of **James T**, sometime tacksman at Mill of Knockando, residing in Mortlick, 16 Jun 1781 and 11 May 1782.

THOMSON, JAMES, senior, see **James Thomson**.

THOMSON, JAMES, merchant in Aberdeen, 14 Mar 1797.

THOMSON, JAMES, lately cashier to the Commercial Banking Company in Aberdeen, 27 Nov 1800.

THOMSON, JEAN, resident in Aberdeen, 2 May 1782.

THOMSON, JOHN, dyer at Waukmiln of Forgue, 9 Apr 1767.

THOMSON, JOHN, Capt, residing in Aberdeen, 5 Mar 1779.

THOMSON, JOHN, mariner in Aberdeen, 8 Mar 1786.

THOMSON, JOHN, sometime in Howboat, 18 Feb 1800.

THOMSON, MARGARET, resident in Aberdeen, 3 Jul 1762.

THOMSON, MARGARET, wife of late **James Griach**, in Coutlach, 22 Nov 1787.

THOMSON, MARGARET, sometime servant to Lord Aboyne, afterwards residing in Kirktoun of Aboyne, 8 Feb 1798.

THOMSON, MARGARET, only daughter of late **Andrew T** of Banchory, 14 Jan 1800.

THOMSON, ROBERT, porter or residenter in Aberdeen, 11 Nov 1783.

THOMSON, WILLIAM, in Inver of Monymusk, 17 Jan 1766.

TILLERAY, WILLIAM, farmer in Aberdeen, 24 Jun 1795.

TOASH, MARGARET, residing in Aberdeen, 17 Jul 1794.

TOCHER, GEORGE, in Newbyth, 23 Mar 1786.

TOURNIER, CHEVALIER, see **Isobel Duncan**.

TOWER, JOHN, junior, merchant in Aberdeen, 24 Jan 1777 and 3 Jun 1782.

TRAILL, JOHN, gardener in Aberdeen,   See **Margaret Massie**.

TROUP, GEORGE, salmon-fisher at Ruthrieston.   See **Jean Williamson**.

TROUP, JOHN, in Mains of Pittrichie, 21 Apr 1767.

THOMSON, ALEXANDER, see **Katharine Skene**.

THOMSON, MARGARET, see **James Griach**.

TURNBULL, PETER, landwaiter at port of Aberdeen, 30 May 1763.

TURNER, GEORGE, of Menie, 30 Jun 1773.

TURNER, MARY, Mrs, wife of late Mr **William Smith**, Episcopal minister, residing in Aberdeen, 23 May 1775.

TURNER, ROBERT, Sheriff-Substitute of Aberdeenshire, 24 Feb 1794.

TYTLER, GEORGE, see **Harry Tytler**.

TYTLER, HARRY, merchant in Milltown of Corsindae, and **George T**, his son, 22 Apr 1782.

TYTLER, JOHN, in Milntown of Corsindae, 9 Feb 1762.

TYTLER, JOHN, late of Brompton, Middlesex, gardener, afterwards at Gilcomstone, 1 Oct 1800.

UDNY, ALEXANDER, Esq of Udny, 2 Dec 1789, 4 Jan 1792 and 31 Jul 1799.

UDNY, THOMAS, Mr, minister at Strichen, 12 Nov 1782.

URQUHART, ANNE, Mrs, widow of **Charles Gordon**, of Blelack, 14 Jan 1799.

URQUHART, KEITH, of Meldrum, Esq, 21 Jun 1793.

URQUHART, PATRICK, merchant in Fraserburgh, 20 Jun 1783.

URQUHART, WILLIAM, merchant and late bailie in Fraserburgh, 19 Mar 1776.

VOLUM, JEAN, residing in Peterhead, widow of **James Hector**, mason in Aberdeen, 28 Oct 1799.

WALKER, ALEXANDER, late provost of Aberdeen, see **Helen Irvine**.

WALKER, ALEXANDER, thread dyer near the Well of Spaw, 17 Oct 1777.

WALKER, ALEXANDER, merchant in Aberdeen, 3 Feb 1798 (1797).

WALKER, ALEXANDER, see **John Walker**.

WALKER, ELSPET, widow of **James Ritchie**, sometime in Kintocher, parish of Lumphanan, 4 Jul 1782.

WALKER, GEORGE, sometime advocate in Aberdeen, thereafter landwaiter at the port thereof, 3 Sep 1772.

WALKER, JAMES, Mr, minister at Peterhead, 19 Apr and 15 Jun 1763.

WALKER, JAMES, see **Christian Forbes**.

WALKER, JOHN, only son of **Alexander W** in Lynn of Culter, 26 Nov 1762.

WALKER, MARGARET, in Peterhead, 15 Nov 1764.

WALKER, MARY, resident in Aberdeen, 21 Apr 1779.

WALKER, MARY, widow of **George Shand**, late in Aberdeen, sometime in Demerara, 28 Sep 1793.

WALKER, PATRICK, merchant in Aberdeen, 31 Jan 1780.

WALKER, WILLIAM, dyer in Aberdeen, 18 Jul 1766.

WALKER, WILLIAM, porter or labourer in Aberdeen, 13 Jan 1794.

WALLACE, ALEXANDER, butcher in Aberdeen, 4 Dec 1795.

WALLACE, JOHN, in Cothill, parish of Slains, 17 Jun 1791.

WATSON, JAMES, advocate in Aberdeen, 13 Jul 1797, 2 Feb and 21 Dec 1798.

WATSON, JEAN, in Torrencroy, 1 Dec 1768.

WATSON, WILLIAM, late farmer in Whitehall, parish of Tyrie, see **Margaret Largoe**.

WATSON, WILLIAM, late merchant in Banff, 4 Mar 1797.

WATT, GEORGE, merchant in Aberdeen, 8 Jan 1768.

WATT, GEORGE, late in Mains of Cairnbulg, 28 Dec 1791.

WATT, JOHN, in Hill of Clune, 30 Aug 1764.

WATT, JOHN, in Haugh, 13 Apr 1785.

WATT, JOHN, sometime wright in Dalkeith, afterwards in Edinburgh, last in Aberdeen, 4 Jul 1798.

WATT, JOHN, see **Marjory Galloway**.

WATT, PATRICK, vintner in Aberdeen, 21 Feb 1791.

WATT, WILLIAM, son of late **William W** at Walkmilne of Strichen, 29 Apr 1794.

WEBSTER, ALEXANDER, sometime in Tarland, see **Barbara Gillenders**.

WEBSTER, GEORGE, sometime in Collarlie, 26 Oct 1792.

WEBSTER, JAMES, see **Helen Leslie**.

WEBSTER, JOHN, late at Mills of Fraserburgh, thereafter in Cross-burntland, 1 Feb 1772(1).

WEBSTER, WILLIAM, in Tiftie, 1 Dec 1763.

WEBSTER, WILLIAM, sometime in Mill of Hole, thereafter in Hardgate of Aberdeen, 21 Apr 1778.

WEIR, ROBERT, gardener in Portsoy, 24 Jun 1782.

WESTLAND, ROBERT, smith, in Bents of Balblair, 17 Feb 1780.

WEY, JANET, resident in Aberdeen, 21 Jul 1785.

WHITE, JANET, widow of **William Mitchell**, sometime in Mains of Artamford, 3 Dec 1772.

WHITE, PATRICK, tidesman in Peterhead, 2 May 1777.

WHITE, WILLIAM, Capt, shipmaster in Peterhead, 14 Jun 1792.

WILDGOOSE, ALEXANDER, see **James Wildgoose**.

WILDGOOSE, JAMES, in Meikletoun of Slains, son of **Alexander W**, in Ward of Slains, 29 Feb 1776.

WILDGOOSE, JEAN, sometime in Adie, thereafter in Hillhead of Bellscamphy, 15 Mar 1768.

WILLIAM, PETER, shoemaker in Craigielae, 30 Aug 1793.

WILLIAMSON, ALEXANDER, late of the Island of Jamaica, last at Haugh of Edinglassie, 23 Dec 1791.

WILLIAMSON, ALEXANDER, in Haugh of Edinglassie, 27 Aug 1796.

WILLIAMSON, JAMES, butcher in Aberdeen, 30 Nov 1767.

WILLIAMSON, JEAN, widow of **George Troup**, salmonfisher at Ruthrieston, 30 Nov 1785.

WILLISON, THOMAS, ship carpenter in Banff, 12 May 1767.

WILLOX, GEORGE, late merchant in Old Aberdeen, 2 May 1800.

WILLOX, ROBERT, Mr, minister at Echt, 12 Sep 1765.

WILLOX, THOMAS, mariner on board the *Ariadne* of Aberdeen, 20 Oct 1800.

WILSON, ALEXANDER, in Knowie Muir, 21 Apr 1775.

WILSON, ALEXANDER, in Cullen, factor to Earl of Findlater, 6 Jun 1789.

WILSON, ALEXANDER, see **Margaret Wilson**.

WILSON, ARCHIBALD, late hecklemaker in Aberdeen, 29 Jan 1783.

WILSON, DAVID, Dr, late of Finzeauch, physician in Peterhead, 15 Nov 1791.

WILSON, ELIZABETH, widow of Mr **Alexander Strachan**, late minister at Keig, 29 Mar 1791.

WILSON, JAMES, in Culphin, parish of Boyndie, 17 Dec 1783.

WILSON, MARGARET, daughter of **Alexander W** of Fornest, merchant in Fraserburgh, 29 Jun 1769.

WILSON, MARGARET, resident in Aberdeen, widow of **David Rattray**, confectioner there, 4 Jan 1794.

WISE, WILLIAM, merchant in Aberdeen, 18 Apr 1769.

WISEMAN, JAMES, late Lt Col of 91st Regiment of Foot, residing in Banff, 25 Jul 1800.

WISHART, JEAN, residing in Aberdeen, 12 Dec 1791.

WOOD, SARAH, widow of **Adam Panton**, merchant in Banff, 9 Mar 1762.

WYLIE, ANDREW, barber in Aberdeen, see **Elizabeth Allan**.

WYNESS, JOHN, in Oldtown of Balquhyne, 31 Mar 1761.

YEATS, JEAN, Mrs, widow of **James Garden**, merchant in Aberdeen, thereafter wife of **Andrew Gray**, merchant in Aberdeen, 27 Nov 1772.

YOUNG, JAMES, merchant in Aberdeen, 12 Jul 1787.

YOUNG, JOHN, merchant in Aberdeen, 10 Mar 1789.

YOUNG, WILLIAM, senior, merchant in Aberdeen, 24 Apr 1780.

YULE, ALEXANDER, in Houseahill, 1 Nov 1790.

ZUCKERT, CHRISTIAN, of Queen Street, Golden Square, in parish of St James, in Liberty of Westminster and county of Middlesex, widow, lately residing in Aberdeen, 4 Dec 1792.